"Very infrequently, a scientist comes along whose work leads to a quantum change in the quality and significance of research in some field. Such a scientist is William Bengston, who is responsible for such a change in the recondite field of anomalous healing. His results are so extraordinary as to eclipse all previous work in that field. Bengston would be a prime candidate for a Nobel Prize in Alternative Medicine, if such an award existed."

—PETER STURROCK, emeritus professor of applied physics at Stanford University

"Great advances in science and medicine often occur at the edge of knowledge, where things don't fit in. Often the misfits are dismissed by conventional thinkers without a hearing. Where William Bengston's work is concerned, this would be a profound mistake, because many precise scientific studies now confirm that healers and healing are real. Somewhere along the line, physicians forgot how to heal, and 'healing' became an embarrassment. Bengston is a harbinger of a marvelous trend: the return of healing to medicine."

—LARRY DOSSEY, MD, author of *Healing Words*

"I believe that energy healing's time will come in the next ten years and that William Bengston's work will be seen as a milestone in that process. We're already experiencing a meltdown of faith in materialistic systems, and that includes the grip of the profit-driven pharmaceutical industry on medical practice."

—EDWARD MANN, Canadian sociologist and energy healing historian

D1016690

"Bill Bengston is a criminologist, sociologist, statistician, college professor, cancer researcher, energy healer. An expert in all these fields! I have been in Bill's orbit observing him engage others in rich dialogue. The consistent effect of his thesis of life challenges even brilliant minds to rethink their foundational assumptions. Bill's mesmerizing memoir reads like a novel."

—FRANCESCA MCCARTNEY, doctor of energy medicine, founder and president of Energy Medicine University, author of *Body of Health: The New Science of Intuition Medicine*®

"Professor William Bengston is shaking the foundations of medical research. What is at stake is the entire clinical trial process. In carefully carried-out experiments, Professor Bengston showed dramatic healing of cancer tumors in mice using energy medicine. By tracing the path of healing intention, he has found that it follows surprising turns and is not easy to control. The simple model of a controlled study does not work in medicine. Bengston's story is one of breakthrough discoveries and a fascinating tale that is not yet complete."

—GARRET MODDEL, professor of electrical engineering, Department of Electrical, Computer, and Energy Engineering, University of Colorado

"Bill Bengston has all the creds and talent to make it bigtime in mainstream academia, but he also has the guts to stick to what he sees and knows, and tell us about it, even if it is way out of the box. Here we have his very exciting adventures in healing, with decidedly anomalous results.

It is to Bill's great credit that he tells it like it is and sustains the contact with this mind-bending material so that it is neither distorted, ignored, or blown out of proportion. Really excellent work!"

—RICHARD A. BLASBAND, MD, former faculty member of Yale Medical School

"Bengston's research on the healing of cancer in mice is an eye-opener, both for its direct implications and for what it says about the difficulty of gaining acceptance for unconventional results, no matter how well documented. His methodology is clear, his results are unambiguous, and several experiments strongly suggest that his healing technique is teachable. Whether you're a healer, a doctor, a biologist, or simply an interested citizen, you owe it to yourself to find out what Bill has been learning over the last two decades."

—YORK DOBYNS, physicist, Princeton University

the
Energy
Cure

the
Energy
Cure

Unraveling the Mystery
of Hands-On Healing

William Bengston, PhD
with Sylvia Fraser

SOUNDS TRUE
Boulder, Colorado

Sounds True, Inc.
Boulder, CO 80306

Copyright © 2010 William Bengston and Sylvia Fraser

Sounds True is a trademark of Sounds True, Inc.

All rights reserved. No part of this book may be used or reproduced in any manner
without written permission from the author and publisher.

This work is solely for personal use and education. The contents of this book are the opinion of its author. The author has a PhD in sociology and is not a medical doctor or other
licensed health-care professional. The instructions and methods presented herein are in
no way intended to be the only method of treatment for a particular ailment and are not
a substitute for medical or psychological treatment from licensed health-care professionals. The author and publisher strongly advise each reader to seek professional advice as
appropriate before making any health decision. The application of protocols and information in this book is the choice of each reader, who assumes full responsibility for his or
her understandings, interpretations, and results. The author and publisher assume no
responsibility or liability whatsoever for the actions or choices of any reader. The creators,
producers, and distributors of this book disclaim any liability or loss in connection with
the ideas herein. Any stories or testimonials presented in this book do not constitute a warranty, guarantee, or prediction regarding the outcome of an individual using the Bengston
Energy Healing Method™ for any particular issue. Every effort has been made to contact
the individuals who are mentioned or quoted in this book. Any questions about permissions should be directed to the Permissions Department at Sounds True: 413 S. Arthur
Ave., Louisville, CO 80027

To protect the privacy of people mentioned in this book, some names have been changed.

Cover and book design by Rachael Murray

Photos © William Bengston

Printed in Canada

Library of Congress Cataloging-in-Publication Data
Bengston, William.
  The energy cure : unraveling the mystery of hands-on healing / by
  William Bengston with Sylvia Fraser.
       p. ; cm.
  Includes bibliographical references.
  ISBN 978-1-59179-911-5 (pbk.)
  1. Touch—Therapeutic use. I. Fraser, Sylvia. II. Title.
  [DNLM: 1. Therapeutic Touch—Personal Narratives. WB 890 B466e 2011]
  RZ999.B464 2011
  615.8'51—dc22
                              2010007772

E-Book ISBN: 978-1-59179-968-9

10 9 8 7 6 5 4 3 2

This book is dedicated to all those who have sought to push intellectual boundaries through rigorous scientific inquiry.

"It has often appeared, while I have been soothing my patients, as if there were some strange property in my hands to pull and draw away from the afflicted parts aches and diverse impurities."

—HIPPOCRATES, the father of medicine

"A new scientific truth does not triumph by convincing its opponents and making them see the light, but rather because its opponents eventually die and a new generation grows up that is familiar with it."

—MAX PLANCK, the father of quantum physics

Contents

Acknowledgments

I FIRST MET SYLVIA FRASER at a workshop I was giving in Toronto. She had been told about the workshop by a mutual sociologist/friend, Ted Mann. Someone there had warned me to be careful with my delivery because "there may be a reporter in the audience," though I wasn't sure what to be worried about. In any event, before the opening talk Sylvia introduced herself to me, and asked if it was okay to record the workshop. I agreed. About an hour into the talk, I mentioned to the audience that the data I was about to discuss had not yet been published, and so I requested that they exercise discretion. The next thing I heard was the click of Sylvia turning off her tape recorder. I was impressed.

A few weeks after the workshop, Sylvia approached me with an offer to cowrite a book on my "story." She said that she believed it was an important story, and that I "could" write it, but probably wouldn't. She also said that if I wrote it in my academic style, no one would read it! And so a partnership was born.

It has been a wonderful partnership. Sylvia is a professional par excellence. In addition to her obvious talents as a wordsmith (eleven books to her credit), she is focused, detail oriented, and persistent. The many hours we spent in interviews passed not only painlessly, but were actually enjoyable. Her mastery of the many facts and chronologies that went into the writing of this book was impressive, to say the least. If I ever need to know anything about myself . . . well, you get the picture. And so for whatever may come of this venture, Sylvia must be acknowledged as the prime mover of this book. I am deeply grateful for her integrity and commitment to the research described here.

There are so many people who have shared the ongoing journey about which you will read in this book that it is impossible to credit them all. And so, in advance, apologies to those omitted, and pardon to those mentioned who might have preferred anonymity. The most obvious person to acknowledge is Bennett Mayrick, who despite the occasional turbulence reported here, is clearly among the dominant influences in my life. His talent and uniqueness have had a profoundly lasting effect on me. I have also recently reconnected with Ben's son Stuart, who has generously provided insight and illumination about his dad. Appreciation also goes out to the people who have been treated by the techniques reported here. All their names have been changed to protect their privacy, but their obvious courage has often inspired me and helped me understand the complexities of the alternative medicine world.

I would like to emphatically thank those who have helped me in my pursuit of data and research, which I consider to be the most fundamental part of this story. I was first introduced to quality research on healing by reading the incredible pioneering work of Bernard Grad. All of us who do research in healing should forever be grateful to the path he blazed at McGill University against enormous opposition. He will always be the "Great Grad" to me, in addition to becoming my friend and supporter.

Dave Krinsley, friend and geologist, set up and funded the initial cancer experiments reported here. Without him, my story would be very different. It was also Dave Krinsley who introduced me to the Society for Scientific Exploration, which has become the central base from which I have reported my ongoing research. That society, founded several decades ago by some pioneering scientists, remains an oasis for serious scientists unafraid of bringing rigorous methods to the study of anomalies. Peter Sturrock (astrophysics, Stanford University), Bob Jahn (engineering, Princeton University), Ian Stevenson (psychiatry, University of Virginia), to name a few of the founders, serve as role models for scientific bravery.

Already eminent in traditional fields, they were unafraid of pushing the boundaries.

I cannot overstate what a breath of fresh air the Society for Scientific Exploration has been for me and hundreds of other scientists. At the annual meetings I have been enriched by the challenges and encouragement of so many people, including (alphabetically) Marsha Adams, Imants Baruss, Henry Bauer, K. C. Blair, Richard Blasband, John Bockris, Stephen Braude, Courtney Brown, Eugene Carpenter, Adam Curry, James DeMeo, York Dobyns, Larry Dossey, Brenda Dunne, Tom Dykstra, Laurence Fredrick, Bruce Greyson, Jay Gunkelman, Bernard Haisch, Nand Harjani, Luke Hendricks, Elissa Hoeger, Patrick Huyghe, Robert Jahn, Joie Jones, David Krinsley, Yury Kronn, Dave Leiter, John MacLean, Ted Mann, Francesca McCartney, Carl Medwedeff, Garret Moddel, Margaret Moga, Roger Nelson, Jan Petersen, Rosemarie Pilkington, Dean Radin, John Reed, Glen Rein, Beverly Rubik, Lev Sadovnik, Savely Savva, Rupert Sheldrake, Richard Shoup, Nancy Smoot, Peter Sturrock, Maria Syldona, Charles Tolbert, Chantal Toporow, Mark Urban-Lurain, John Valentino, Harald Walach, Mike Wilson, and Bob Wood. Thank you, all. I can only hope that I have given you something back.

The research reported here has been sponsored by a variety of institutions. In temporal order, I'd like to thank Queens College of the City University of New York, coordinated by David Krinsley and Marv Wasserman; St.

Joseph's College, coordinated by Carol Hayes; Arizona State University, coordinated by David Krinsley; the University of Connecticut Medical Center, coordinated by Pramod Srivastava; and the Indiana University School of Medicine, coordinated by Margaret Moga and Roy Geib. Obvious thanks also go out to the skeptical student volunteers who had their worldviews shaken by the research.

A special thanks goes to St. Joseph's College, New York. In an era when scientific orthodoxy reigns supreme and researchers can be blackballed for challenging the status quo, St. Joseph's College has been consistently supportive of my efforts. While I may be viewed as a bit eccentric because of my research interests, the administration of the college has supported me with sabbaticals, faculty small grants, and even reduced teaching loads. My department, a bit quirky in its own right, has also been tolerant and immensely supportive. I am grateful for their collective generosity.

On a personal note, I would also like to single out Don Murphy, a biologist friend, formerly with the National Institutes of Health, who has a rare combination of intelligence, integrity, and open-mindedness. His selfless advice to me over the past several years has been invaluable. We have published an article together on the question of whether healing can be taught, and have collaborated on a number of research projects that will be reported in the near future.

On the home front, I would like to thank my kids, Brian and Liz, for putting up with, and even encouraging, the passions of their strange dad! Ditto for my sister and brother, and their spouses and families.

Finally, on the most personal note, I would like to dedicate this book to my wife, Joann—my intellectual muse, chief supporter, and best friend. She is the love of my life.

—*William Bengston*

THE BREAKTHROUGH RESEARCH IN THIS book, the fascinating story, and the charismatic voice all belong to Bill Bengston. My enjoyable task was to bring this seminal work to as broad a public as possible, in as timely a fashion as possible.

Vital to this enterprise are Bruce Westwood, Carolyn Forde, and Natasha Daneman of Westwood Creative Artists; editor Haven Iverson and contracts administrator Jaime Schwalb, and the rest of the energetic Sounds True team.

A special thanks to Anna and Julian Porter for their support, advice, and enduring friendship.

—*Sylvia Fraser*

Introduction

OVER THE PAST THIRTY-FIVE YEARS I have successfully treated many types of cancer—bone, pancreatic, breast, brain, rectal, lymphatic, stomach, leukemia—as well as other diseases, all using a hands-on technique that is painless, noninvasive, and has no unpleasant side effects. To my knowledge, no person I have healed ever experienced a recurrence.

The effectiveness of this treatment has now been proven in ten controlled animal-experiments, conducted in five university medical and biological laboratories by trained, skeptical researchers. Though my initial response to the validity of hands-on healing was one of incredulity, the accumulation of replicable scientific data has overwhelmed my own disbelief. I have become a failed skeptic.

By choice and training, I am a sociology professor at St. Joseph's College in New York. Though I try to keep my two lives separate, some spillage inevitably occurs.

About twenty-five years ago, I taught two women in their mid-forties who had raised their families and then returned to the classroom together to earn their BA degrees. In eerie fashion, both Laurie and Carol received the same sobering diagnosis at the same time: breast and lymphatic cancer had metastasized, meaning tumors were spreading throughout their bodies. Each was told by separate doctors that her disease, if left untreated, would kill her in about four months.

Both women were married to professionally successful, conservative men who expected them to take the traditional medical route, which meant radiation and chemotherapy. Laurie, who is very outgoing and persistent, had heard stories of my healing abilities. Against all advice, she opted to be treated by me. I had experienced Laurie's feistiness on our first meeting, when she badgered me into admitting her to one of my sociology courses despite her lack of prerequisite credits. Now she was even more determined to opt for hands-on healing in preference to the harshness of chemotherapy.

For two months I treated Laurie six days a week, sometimes many hours a day. So intense was the process that I developed alarming lumps in my own armpits and groin, which disappeared when I physically disconnected from her. The usual medical tests administered by her doctors, including X-rays, blood work, and CAT scans (three-dimensional body imaging), showed her tumors to be shrinking. Eventually they disappeared.

By then we'd had the sad experience of attending Carol's funeral.

Laurie and I celebrated the fifth and tenth anniversaries of her remaining cancer free. We still keep in touch sporadically, and her husband, who had opposed my treatments, has become a friend and supporter.

In my experience, the people with the best prognosis for a cure are the youthful ones with the most aggressive cancers. Four-year-old Ryan was a cute, bright kid who loved trains and who could name every stop on several Manhattan subway lines. He had been diagnosed with retinoblastoma, a particularly nasty cancer that usually led to removal of one or both eyes, followed by brain tumors and death. By the time his anxious parents brought him to me, he was "medicalized" from having been dragged from doctor to doctor. Even talking about illness made him angry.

When Ryan came into my home, he was pouting and whining like four-year-olds do. I said, "Ryan," then held up my left hand, which is my healing hand. Grabbing it, he laid it against his eye. Then he sat quietly for about an hour while I went through the healing process. About the time I felt the treatment to be completed, Ryan pulled away, reverting to a contrary four-year-old.

That became our little modus operandi for the first four treatments. Even though I thought Ryan was cured, I added a few extra sessions while we awaited test results. Now his parents had to hold him, squirming and protesting, as if he sensed he no longer needed me.

For a couple of years Ryan's mother sent me e-mails, during which she referred to Ryan's recovery as a "fond memory of a magical time."

In dealing with cancer, I have had no failures where my two conditions for success have been met: that the person completes the course of treatment, and that he or she comes to me before having radiation or chemotherapy. My sense is that conventional medical treatments, intended to kill cancerous cells, also destroy something "energetic" in the patients. This, I believe, is diametrically opposed to the nurturing effect created by energy healing. Administering hands-on treatment afterward feels like trying to activate a dead battery.

Though my most dramatic results have been with cancer, I have also cured other diverse conditions. Paul from Michigan was about forty-eight when he contacted me six years ago. A marathon runner, he had been diagnosed with a heart-valve problem requiring surgery. Paul was determined to do whatever it took to avoid an open-heart operation, the thought of which terrified him. Fixing Paul's valve required about five sessions for which he—a goal-directed person—pursued me by car, train, and plane. He still continues to run marathons.

In general, the longer a disease has taken to develop, the longer it takes to cure, much like playing a videotape backward. With diseases such as diabetes, Parkinson's, and arthritis, I have been able to lessen debilitating symptoms by up to 50 percent, but not make the condition go away. My treatment is not faith based. Neither patient nor practitioner is expected to believe in anything, including the process itself, for it to be effective. Nor do I consider hands-on healing to be a replacement for traditional Western medicine. Where I differ from most doctors is in my greater belief in the body's ability to cure itself, often eliminating the need for radical intervention.

I have also discovered through my own research that products dispensed by pharmaceutical companies as tried, tested, and true often owe their advertised benefits to the interpretation of experimental findings rather than to irrefutable facts. Perhaps this is the reason for so many drug recalls due to toxic or unpleasant side effects. This suggests to me that populations into which a drug is introduced are often part of an extended human experiment.

Hands-on healing has the advantage of being completely safe. Its principles underlie Eastern healing practices such as acupuncture and yoga, which are backed by four thousand years of tradition. They are also supported by quantum physics, which describes the material world in terms of energy fields.

I discovered my hands-on ability through a mentor who was a natural healer. We met in Long Island, New York, during the summer of 1971, when I was twenty-one. Though Bennett Mayrick was in his late forties, he had only recently discovered that he had psychic abilities. By his own testimony, he could hold an object belonging to someone he had never met and give detailed information about its owner. In parapsychological literature, that's known as "psychometry." For months I tested him with objects provided by friends, determined either to debunk his alleged abilities or to understand scientifically how they worked. Even when I designed double-blind studies to outfox him, using protocols that I considered flawless, Ben always beat me.

While conducting readings, Ben began to pick up physical sensations corresponding to the medical problems of the object's owner. His initial impulse was to draft me to help him banish these unwelcome effects. Instead, I became his first patient. He cured me of chronic back pain that has never returned.

Through trial and error, Ben morphed into a hands-on healer without either of us knowing what was happening. Through word of mouth, people would come to him with their afflictions. Ben would put his hands on each one, for thirty minutes to an hour, curing or improving conditions previously considered incurable. He had some unexpected failures. He could not make warts disappear, and as far as the common cold is concerned, you'd probably do just as well with an inhaler.

With cancers we would typically learn through blood work and CAT scans that the disease had retreated, then disappeared. Most of our patients' doctors classified these unexpected cures as spontaneous remission, a rare but medically recognized phenomenon. By contrast, we were routinely observing such remissions involving a wide variety of cancers. What was happening in each case? What tied these cases together?

Despite gratifying clinical results, I was growing increasingly frustrated from a scientific viewpoint. Each and every patient came with complex physical and psychological issues that made it difficult to isolate the results of Ben's work. Perhaps one might be taking massive doses of vitamin C, or visiting an acupuncturist, or undergoing more orthodox medical treatments.

As a scientist, this problem confounds me even today. Did the macrobiotic diet Laurie insisted on following have anything to do with her cure? Though Laurie's and Carol's conditions were superficially the same, what were the underlying differences? If I had treated Carol instead of Laurie, would she have survived, or would the results for both have been the same? What, in Laurie's case, were the critical factors leading to a cure?

My relentless need for answers drove me into the controlled world of the laboratory in search of ironclad, replicable validation. Our first experiment was to be conducted with mice in 1975 in the biology department at Queens College of the City University of New York. At the last moment Ben, who abhorred formal testing, refused to participate. Since I had been joint-healing with him for several years, I reluctantly substituted.

In the initial experiment, which became the template, mice bred for research were injected with a particularly lethal strain of mammary cancer that had always resulted in 100 percent fatality within fourteen to twenty-seven days. Through hands-on healing, these results were completely reversed: 100 percent of the mice survived the disease to become cancer free and to live a normal two-year life span! This experiment was replicated once more at Queens College with the same 100 percent success. Eight other replications, with minor variations, at four other biological and medical laboratories produced comparable results. Just as amazing, mice that were re-injected did not get cancer, suggesting they had developed an immunity.

I wish to remind readers that my animal research findings reverse the classic experimental model. I did not begin by testing mice in a lab, producing a theory that now awaits human application. I went into the lab to verify and gain insight into a procedure that I had already successfully used to cure many people of a variety of medical problems, especially cancer.

Admittedly, much remains to be learned about how my treatments work.

- Does hands-on healing kill cancer, or does it stimulate the body's immune system to heal itself?

- Since the mice we cured became immune to further cancer injections, could the blood of cured mice be used to develop a vaccine? Given that my clinical patients have experienced no known recurrence, could the same experimental process be used to produce a cancer vaccine for humans?

- What happens between healer and patient during hands-on treatments? Is energy or information exchanged? How are their brains affected? To try to unlock these secrets, I have been undergoing functional magnetic resonance imaging (fMRIs, which are multilevel scans more detailed than CAT scans) and electroencephalographs (EEGs, which measure the brain's electrical activity) while in healing mode.

More recently, I have directed my curiosity toward a question with broad clinical application: can hands-on healing be learned by others using my techniques? Since most cultures have independently produced a tradition of hands-on healing, it seems reasonable to assume that this ability may be distributed throughout any population, much like artistic or musical talent. If so, how can people who possess this ability uncover and utilize it?

Unraveling the mystery of hands-on healing has been the passion driving much of my work over the past three decades. Like most high-stakes, life-and-death stories, this one has not always proceeded smoothly. Along with exhilarating triumphs, I have encountered perverse roadblocks, strange anomalies, and—most discouraging of all—the arbitrary rejection of hard scientific data on the grounds that it is too good to be true. I have also gained intriguing insights into the complexities of human nature, the tragedy of self-sabotage, and the yawning gap between stated desire and behavior.

That's the adventure—still ongoing—which I will recount in this book.

1. A Remarkable Encounter

"Fiction is obliged to stick to possibilities. Truth isn't."

—MARK TWAIN

IN THE SUMMER OF 1971, when I was twenty-one, I met the man who would change the course of my life. The previous May, I had graduated with a bachelor's degree in sociology from Niagara University in upstate New York, with absolutely no idea what to do next. While buying time, I took a job lifeguarding as I had done for the past few summers, this time at a new pool in Great Neck, Long Island. In hindsight, I was ripe for a conversion experience.

During an otherwise ordinary afternoon, another lifeguard pointed out a man on the pool deck, whom she identified rather sardonically as a psychic. With curiosity piqued, I decided to introduce myself to him during my next break. At that time, I would say I was open-minded to psychic phenomena in principle, but intensely skeptical of those claiming to produce it. As a teenager, I had had a number of dreams around death that had proven startlingly prophetic. This motivated me to read some of the popular paranormal literature, most of which was anecdotal and little of which impressed me. I had also taken a noncredit, adult education course on the paranormal at Buffalo State University, with instructor Douglas Dean, a well-respected parapsychology researcher. In the course, Dean reviewed laboratory experiments, conducted with strict protocols, into such phenomena as telepathy and energy healing. Those did impress me, and I was puzzled as to why so many scientists were hostile toward what appeared to be legitimate results.

Bennett Mayrick was dark haired, had a crooked nose, and was deeply tanned, slightly overweight, and about six foot one. I estimated him to be around fifty years old (in fact, he was forty-eight). Though I had never met a psychic before, I expected him to be full of exaggerated claims, eager to promote himself and to profit from his alleged talent. I couldn't have been more wrong. As we chatted through a couple of my breaks, he made it clear that being a psychic was not a business to him and that he had only recently discovered his abilities. Instead of trying to convince me, he spoke in a soft, very deep voice, as if bemused at my interest. This was definitely not a guy who was selling. Instead, I sensed his profound ambivalence about something that was happening to him that both excited and threatened him.

According to Mayrick, eight months earlier he attended a party where a psychic provided the entertainment. After everyone had thrown a personal object into a box, she withdrew them one at a time, attempting to tell each owner something about him- or herself.

After a few readings, the psychic inexplicably instructed Mayrick to select an item and to tell a story about it. Though he protested he was a nonbeliever, she pressured him until he picked up a ring. Holding it in his palm, he announced that its owner had recently changed jobs. To his surprise, this was confirmed. Mayrick picked up a second object, then invented another story. Again, this was confirmed. As he testified, he did this several more times, growing increasingly elaborate, and each time having the details corroborated.

Though personally unconvinced, I egged him on by asking, "Were you receiving visual images?"

"No. I just blurted out the first thing that came to my mind, feeling like a damned fool!"

He didn't know many of the people at the party, and finally he concluded that everyone, including the psychic, was targeting him as the butt of a joke.

Deciding to take the gag to the next level, Mayrick selected a watch. Holding it in his palm, he related a detailed story about an affair that its owner had carried on, precisely describing the man's lover and the places where they had met. "All of a sudden one of the guys at the party got really red-faced and flustered," reported Mayrick. "Later another guy took me aside to ask how I'd known about the secret affair. Apparently everything I said was true."

Before I could express any skepticism, Mayrick undercut me by expressing his own. "I fully expected I'd get a call the next day from the host of the party telling me I'd been had. Instead, people kept phoning to ask where I got my information. They thought the psychic and I had been in cahoots. Even after several days I still expected a call. When it never came, I started picking up objects and making up stories, trying to figure out what was happening, and waiting for the other shoe to drop."

"You mean the delayed call from your party host?"

"No, waiting to be wrong."

Now I was sure this guy was either grossly exaggerating or deluded. No psychic ever dared to claim 100 percent accuracy. That was unheard of, even among the gullible. At the same time, I was taken aback by how nonchalant Mayrick seemed about his declarations and how uninterested he appeared in whether or not I believed him. The good part, from my point of view, was that he had set himself up to be checkmated.

"Will you do a reading for me?" I asked.

I had expected him to be evasive. Instead, he was ironic. "Sure. Give me something. Maybe I'll finally be wrong."

I handed him my wallet, determined not to offer any verbal or visual clues.

Again, he was one step ahead of me. "Don't tell me anything about yourself. The less I know, the better it works."

While holding my wallet in the palm of his left hand, he smoked with his right one. His eyes—very dark, and clear yet complex—seemed to go out of focus as he said, "I'm sensing anxiety around a woman who's probably in her fifties. She has black, fairly short hair, and she's talking to a younger woman who looks a lot like her—probably it's her daughter. They're expressing concern about a second young woman, this time blonde, who's planning to move to New York."

As Mayrick described how this conversation was supposed to relate to me, I interrupted with some impatience. "You could be talking about my mother and my sister and a friend of mine who may be moving to New York, but the descriptions are too vague to be convincing, and what you claim they're saying isn't characteristic of them."

He refused to backtrack or attempt to reposition himself. "Check it out. It's a conversation that just happened. In the kitchen."

I was profoundly unimpressed. "What else do you get?"

"Something's wrong with your car."

"I just had it inspected. Yesterday. It's fine." I made no effort to hide my disappointment. Some part of me had wanted the excitement of hearing him score with something dramatic. At the same time, I felt that anyone who claimed infallibility deserved to be taken down. I was now quite certain this guy was only an interesting character. "I think you've just heard the other shoe fall," I said.

He remained unfazed. "You'll find I'm right." He was like someone telling you that your birthday is March 14 when you've got a birth certificate—not to mention your own mother—insisting that it's October 6. Clearly, he bought his own stuff.

Partly out of politeness, partly to see how far our resident psychic would go, I asked if he had any other unusual talents.

Without the slightest embarrassment, he made the most absurd claim I had ever heard: "I can dissolve clouds. If I stare through them for a few seconds, they dissipate. Here, I'll show you."

Of course, I knew that some tribal societies claimed to be able to manipulate the weather, which is why "rainmaker" is a popular political metaphor for someone who can change the climate of opinion. What I didn't know is that dissolving clouds is also part of the paranormal literature. Even if I had, I doubt it would have made me any more receptive.

"Pick a cloud," Ben urged.

I refused.

He insisted. "Come on, it's the damnedest thing."

I pointed directly overhead. "That one."

Ben's eyes took on that same unfocused look I'd noticed before. After fifteen or twenty seconds, he announced with satisfaction, "There it goes."

I looked up. The cloud was gone.

"Isn't that something? I only found out a couple of days ago that I can do it."

I picked a second cloud—a medium-sized cumulus floating in isolation against a deep-blue sky. "Try that one."

This time I watched the cloud. After about fifteen seconds, its edges dissolved while its dense center grew transparent. A few moments more and that cloud was also gone, though no others around it were affected.

Mayrick grinned at me while I searched for some plausible explanation. Surely the wind must have blown the clouds apart, or perhaps the sun had created an optical illusion.

"Let's have one more demonstration," I requested, determined to preserve my sense of reality by framing the next experiment. After picking four clouds of similar size and shape, almost touching one another, I put on dark glasses and studied them, memorizing their shapes and textures so completely that to this day I could draw them. "Dissolve only the bottom right one," I instructed.

For the next twenty seconds I strode around the pool, burning into my consciousness the features of the clouds, which had not changed discernibly while I studied them, assuring myself they would remain as I had seen them.

"All finished," announced Mayrick.

When I looked up again, the bottom-right cloud, and only the bottom-right cloud, was gone.

Conceding defeat, I shook his hand. "That's the most amazing thing I've ever seen." Then I walked away, still convinced I had been tricked.

A few hours later, with the psychic all but forgotten, I was half a mile into my commute home when I heard a terrible crash, followed by the scraping of metal on asphalt. The entire exhaust system had fallen out of my car. During the rest of my drive, with the engine spewing smoke, I rationalized away all inclination to credit the psychic: he had not specifically mentioned the exhaust system, and I was in the habit of driving old cars in which mufflers gave out. This one was a 1964 Nova with a replacement red seat because the original had disintegrated.

When I finally arrived home, I found my family in the backyard preparing a barbecue. After cornering my sister, I asked her about the conversation that Mayrick had described between her and our mother.

She was flabbergasted. "How did you find out about that? It was private."

"Where did it take place?"

"In the kitchen."

Under normal circumstances I would have been annoyed at both the inconvenience and the expense of having to fix my car; however, during my morning drive to the garage with it sounding like a tank, I found myself fighting an atypical feeling of exhilaration. The car, the clouds, the kitchen conversation: Mayrick had certainly caught my attention. I was eager to see him again, and since he and his family rented an apartment beside the pool, I didn't have too many days to wait. As soon as I spotted him with his son and daughter on the deck, I sprinted over.

"You were right!" I told him. "My car did break down, and my mother and my sister had the conversation you described."

While I considered this a momentous admission, Ben appeared unmoved. As I would increasingly observe, if I said that the sky was blue and he thought it was green, he would just assume I was color-blind.

On my next break, I peppered him with questions: How did he know something was wrong with my car, but without being able to identify the exhaust system? What was he thinking and feeling as he made his predictions?

While chain-smoking as usual, Ben replied, "When I hold an object, I get an urge to say something, but I don't know what until I hear myself say it. With your wallet, I thought of a car and of trouble. Maybe if I'd held it longer, the idea of the exhaust would have come to me. Maybe not."

That exchange established our relationship for the rest of the summer. I would spend my breaks giving Ben objects from my friends, then questioning him about his answers, which were invariably correct. I was curious. He was flattered. I was also helping to probe a mystery that baffled him.

During Ben's early readings, he would sometimes blurt out very personal information without being able to check himself, just as he had done at the party. With practice, his psychic abilities evolved from an entertainment over which he had little control into a talent that he could channel and even direct. As he described this new process to me: "I'm finding I can scan for information—to be active instead of just waiting for it to find me."

"About anything?"

"I don't know. I've just discovered I could do this."

From time to time Ben gave me impromptu readings, with that familiar faraway look but without needing to hold an object. "You feel you're different and I believe you are. You also sense things you have no business knowing. And you don't believe anyone can fully understand you."

I changed the subject. "What do your friends think about your talent?"

"Most take it as a joke. Some say they always thought I was different."

Since Ben had kept his psychic abilities hidden from himself for so long, we speculated about how many other people were "weird" without knowing it. One of our lifeguards—I'll call her Amelia—came from a large Irish Catholic family that lived in my neighborhood. I used to imagine her very likable mother as a closet witch who was trying hard to live a conventional life. The kids were also very artistic and sensitive, and probably psychic.

I particularly remember Amelia playing around with tarot cards.

Ben put Amelia into a hypnotic regression—something I had never seen him do before—taking her back to age two. It was fascinating to watch her voice and her gestures change. In one incident, she was talking about being lost, and because I was familiar with the neighborhood, I knew exactly where she was, even though she didn't.

After that Amelia was so shaken she didn't want anything more to do with Ben—a common response to his uncanny accuracy as I soon discovered. Whenever we came upon it in the future, we called it the Amelia Effect. It disturbed me at the time, and still does, though I no longer find it unexpected. Were people genuinely not interested, or did they fear the implications of Ben's talent? Did they sense some echoing strangeness in themselves? I suppose that question has a flip side: Why was I so obsessed? Did Ben draw upon an inner yearning of which I was only dimly aware?

It wasn't just Ben's psychic talent that surprised me during the summer of '71. His personal life also had its unpredictable elements, including his occupation.

"I'm a maid," he told me. This translated into cleaning houses with a partner—one of a string of jobs into which he had drifted, including laborer, tradesman, semiprofessional basketball player, even professional singer. Each seldom lasted longer than six months, while earning him just enough to pay rent on the apartment he shared with his wife and two children, run a clunky car, and support his three-pack-a-day smoking addiction. It was a cash business, keeping him afloat on the fringes of society, outside of all systems. He probably didn't even pay taxes.

Sometime in the past, Ben had earned a college degree from Emory and Henry College, in Virginia. He had also served in the U.S. Army during World War II, which was where he first discovered he might be different. When a truck in which he was riding hit a land mine and exploded, he felt himself sail up into the air in slow-motion, then do a backflip before landing safely on both feet. All around him was carnage. Instinctively, he knew his escape had not been normal.

Throughout August, my enthusiasm over Ben's abilities never diminished. I faced the seasonal closing of the pool on Labor Day with a sense of loss, both because of the likely end of our relationship and because I hadn't made any contingency life plan.

Unexpectedly, Ben offered me a job—apparently his cleaning partner had quit. I accepted. So this is where my own biography takes an unexpected twist. I, too, became a maid.

About the same time, I decided to apply to take my master's in sociology at St. John's University in New York City, beginning in January. People, especially parents, can tolerate the eccentric behavior of a graduate student more easily than that of an overeducated semivagrant, and I frankly had no idea what else to do with my life. After considering psychology, I chose sociology. The behavior of groups seemed far more important than how individuals like me conduct, or misconduct, our lives.

2. Maid to Order

"If we watch ourselves honestly we shall often find that we have begin to argue against a new idea even before it has been completely stated."

—**WILFRED TROTTER,** British neurosurgeon

I WASN'T VERY GOOD AT BEING A MAID, even after my five-minute intensive training course. The way Ben and I worked things out was that he would do the heavy lifting in the bathrooms and kitchens while I dusted and vacuumed. This ruse of cleaning allowed me to spend more time with him, while my application to graduate school acted as a sop to those who expected more of me, especially since I was supposed to be intellectually gifted.

Certainly, not much in my conventional background suggested my current interest in the paranormal or in housekeeping. I was born in New York City in 1950—the middle kid with a sister, Lynn, who's three years older, and a brother, Rob, who's six years younger. My father, Earl, was a treasurer or comptroller for department stores and advertising firms. My mother, Norma, looked after the house and family as was standard for the times. Economically we were comfortable, but certainly not rich.

My upbringing was very hands-off as judged by the current yardstick. Douglaston, the most eastern borough of New York City, was an upper-middle-class fantasyland of friendliness where no one locked their doors and you could walk in and out of people's houses most of the time. It was also dynamic, in that high achievement was an unspoken expectation. From that peninsula on Little Neck Bay on Long Island Sound came world-class athletes like tennis great John McEnroe, an inordinate number of successful professionals, and more than our share of suicides and drug overdoses.

Though my parents weren't demanding or materialistic, my conspicuous lack of recognizable ambition was straining their tolerance. With increasing frequency my father would gently inquire where all of this might be leading. With feigned surprise, I asked why he wasn't excited about Ben's incredible abilities. Though Pa never wavered in his lack of interest, neither did he question my right to be obsessed. As someone born into the Depression, and of the first generation in his family to attend college, he had been motivated by a need for economic mobility. Some part of him wanted me to have the freedom he'd never had—but as a maid?

My mother's problem in reconciling herself to my choices came from the fact that she'd never seen me with a dust mop in hand. Her chief worry, however, emanated from her perception that Ben was mad. Though I sometimes wondered if I should be concerned about their concern, deeper than logic was my conviction that I was doing what I was supposed to be doing. Ben was a charismatic, and like all such figures he attracted selectively. Those who fell under his spell and those who didn't felt sorry for each other. Neither my family nor my friends liked Ben or his influence on me, which I was at a loss to explain to them.

As for the job of maid itself, I soon discovered that time meant little to Ben. When he said "morning," it could mean anywhere between nine a.m. and three p.m. Usually I would arrive at his place around 11:30, and maybe he would be up, and eventually we would go to a house and start cleaning. Our conversations ranged from details about the readings he was now doing on a regular basis, to politics and cosmology. He seemed to like having me around, partly because I was better informed in an academic way and partly because my curiosity about his odd talent gave him hope that together we might stumble on the right answers. Or at least the right questions.

My faulty cleaning skills gave Ben yet another reason for tolerating me. I lost him most of his clients about the time he was ready to phase himself out from the business.

Some of the extracurricular activities to which Ben introduced me were as out of character for me as house cleaning. One was horse racing, a sport that enthralled him. After decades of devotion, Ben claimed that he had worked out a mathematical system for beating the odds. While there would be losing races and losing days, there would never be a losing week. If you bet $2 and kept to the system while upping the ante, you would always be ahead at least $20 by the end of the week.

I'm not a gambler; I don't enjoy anything about it, including winning. It was the numbers part of Ben's system that hooked me. After checking eight weeks of old racing forms, I found that, sure enough, he seemed to be right. Now, the system had built-in restrictions about the races on which you could bet. I would do the math, revealing that we should be betting on, say, the third horse in the fourth race. Trouble was, one of us would always come up with some reason for not betting on that horse: it had only "three legs," meaning it had never won, or its jockey didn't seem to know the horse's front end from the back, so we would skip that race, and of course the horse would win. Neither of us developed any learning curve at all about this. It was as if we were in a competition to sabotage each other, so we would usually finish each week with the system having won while we lost.

Many years later Ben's son, who became a psychologist, told me that he thought his father was driven by both the fear of failure and the fear of success. That would explain Ben's ambivalent behavior. I still can't explain mine.

Our partnership also gave me an opportunity to persuade Ben to do things that were out of character for him. This included allowing me to drag him to a couple of parapsychological laboratories to have his psychic abilities tested.

At first, he refused. "Any test they try on me will be meaningless."

I persisted—"How do you know?"

"Believe me, I know."

When Ben finally did agree, it was with conditions. "First, I don't want to be tested on machines; second, any object they give me for a reading has to be something they know a lot about."

Our first stop was the venerable American Society for Psychical Research (ASPR), located on West 73rd Street in Manhattan. It was founded in 1885 by such luminaries as Harvard psychologist William James to investigate the then-popular phenomenon of mediumship. Over the next several decades, it had reinvented itself along the scientific lines pioneered by J. B. Rhine of Duke University. Rhine, a botanist, had become interested in extrasensory perception (ESP), which he defined as the apparent ability to acquire information in ways other than through the known five senses. He also coined the term "parapsychology" to describe the study of this phenomenon.

In the 1930s, Rhine established America's first para-psychological laboratory for the purpose of measuring ESP through precise statistical probabilities. In his most famous test, he asked subjects to guess the order of a pack of randomly shuffled cards, marked with five symbols, obtaining astronomically high odds-against-chance that supported psychic phenomena.

Ben's appointment was for ten o'clock one morning in October. Since that was earlier than he liked to get up, he sulked all the way on the train into Manhattan.

The ASPR is housed in a beautiful, large, four-story brownstone just off Central Park West. Once inside, our first stop was a laboratory full of machines of all shapes and sizes. Noting my curiosity, one of the technicians pointed to a small one. "That's an automated clairvoyance tester. A random generator picks one of four lights, and the subject tries to predict which one it will be. It automatically keeps track of the hits and misses."

He pointed to another. "That's for testing psychokinesis, the ability of the mind to affect matter. Inside is a small piece of radioactive matter that decays according to the laws of quantum mechanics while the test subject tries to speed up or slow down the rate."

Ben interjected. "I can do that."

I turned to him. "I thought you didn't want to be tested on any machines."

"I don't. I simply said I could do that."

Despite Ben's antipathy toward machines, he had agreed to be hooked up to an electroencephalograph (EEG) since it wouldn't be testing his abilities, just monitoring his brain waves. I knew from the parapsychological literature that normal waking consciousness produces beta brain waves of 15 or more cycles per second; alpha is a relaxed state producing 7 to 13 cycles per second; theta produces 4 to 7 cycles; while delta, characterized by deep, dreamless sleep, produces only 1.5 to 4 cycles. At that time, psychic experiences were presumed to occur in the alpha range, and mystical experiences in the theta range.

Ben was to be tested by Karlis Osis, then director of the ASPR, well-known for his extensive study of out-of-body experiences, animal telepathy, and deathbed visions. When I made the appointment with Osis, I explained Ben's main condition: he should only be tested on an item with a well-known history. Given the fact that replication is the biggest problem bedeviling ESP research, Osis was startled at my insistence that Ben could perform with 100 percent accuracy under any circumstances. No doubt he had heard dozens of grandiose claims that had failed to deliver under test conditions.

Osis's questioning of Ben as he was being hooked up on the EEG was very offhand, signaling that he too had become a skeptic in a field that invites skepticism. Afterward he handed Ben a plain brown box, about one foot square, giving no sensory clue to the object inside that Ben was supposed to read.

Despite the wires attached to his scalp, Ben's eyes unfocused in the usual dreamy manner as he explained, "This was a gift that passed through many hands. I see mountains and a small village. South America. Peru. It was purchased by a man about thirty years old. He gave it to a younger woman with brown hair and brown eyes. She gave it to an older man to thank him for a favor. Something about a letter of recommendation." Ben looked at Osis. "That older man was you, but this object isn't very close to you. I'll bet you don't even know what I'm talking about."

Osis was taken aback. "Would you like to know what the object is?"

Ben sighed. "It doesn't matter."

It mattered to me, so I was glad when Osis opened the box. "It's a letter opener, and yes, it was a gift to me from a woman for my recommendation, but I don't think you're right about the South American part. All in all, a promising beginning."

Ben glared at Osis. "You don't even know about the other things."

"No, but if the South American part were true, I'd know."

When Osis turned his attention to the EEG technician, I discreetly picked up the letter opener. It was stamped "Made in Peru."

The technician seemed to be having problems with Ben's EEG printout. "I'm not sure what happened," he told Osis. "A few seconds after you gave Ben the box, his beta activity increased rather than decreased. Then a portion of his occipital lobe started to generate theta waves, which is impossible."

Osis agreed: "Theta is a very diminished state of brain activity. You can't have theta with an active beta."

"Something must be wrong with the machine," said the technician.

"Yes," agreed Osis, checking his watch. "I'm sorry, but I have to go to another appointment. It was a pleasure to meet you, Mr. Mayrick."

Still perplexed, the technician tried the EEG machine on himself. It functioned perfectly. We persuaded Ben to do another reading while hooked up to the machine. Ben again generated beta and theta. The assistant hooked it back to himself. Fine. Then to Ben. Same beta-theta readings. Again, this was attributed to malfunction. Years up the road I discovered that some Indian yogis and Buddhist monks meditate by hyping their brain activity rather than slowing it down, reaching previously unknown gamma states in which fast-slow brain waves are synthesized.

Frustrated by the technician's refusal to take Ben's readings seriously, I suggested that we try a different kind of machine—the one that tests a subject's ability to affect the speed at which radioactive matter decays.

Ben reluctantly agreed. After checking this machine's function, the technician instructed Ben, "Just concentrate on making the radioactive material disintegrate more rapidly."

Ben seemed amused. "No problem."

As Ben sat without even looking at the machine, the technician gave a yelp. "Something's wrong! This thing says the decay is occurring faster than I believe can be possible."

Ben playfully replied, "Then I'll slow it down."

Soon the technician was mumbling something about the decay slowing to almost one-half its normal rate. He turned off the machine. "I don't know what to tell you. Something must be wrong with this one, too."

On the train trip home, Ben was much more vocal. "What did I tell you? It was meaningless. These guys are just as afraid of things that don't fit into their system as the rest!"

I asked him how he had affected the radioactive material.

He perked up. "That was easy. To speed up the decay, I imagined a cloud, which I then dissolved. To slow it down, I imagined a frozen rock."

Ben gave me one more chance to prove to him that parapsychological testing might be useful. This time I took him to the Maimonides Medical Center's Dream Laboratory, in Brooklyn. Once again, I explained in advance that Ben should be tested only on an item with a well-known history. Once again, he was to be monitored by an experienced parapsychological researcher. This turned out to be Charles Honorton, noted for his ESP studies.

After a few soft questions, Honorton handed Ben a scarf for his reading. As soon as Ben touched it, he became agitated. Jumping up, he waved his arms, shouting, "Terror, terror! There's animals all over the place—tigers and elephants and giraffes. I don't get this!" His face was white and he was panting.

"An interesting reading," said Honorton calmly. "The scarf belongs to a girl we think has been abducted. She was last seen at the Bronx Zoo. The police were out of leads so they asked if any of our psychics might help."

Ben threw the scarf at Honorton. "I don't want to do this anymore."

He shouted at me all the way home, which was fine, because I was just as upset. Ben had set only one condition for a reading—that the tester know the history of the target object—and in both cases that protocol had been broken. I had brought these researchers the holy grail—a psychic with astonishing accuracy who never claimed off days—but they were too consumed with their own specialties-of-the-moment to notice.

Unfortunately, I was to find tunnel vision to be the norm across the whole scientific community, and the bigger the picture became, the more certain the experts were to miss it.

3. Breakthrough!

"The philosophies of one age have become the absurdities
of the next, and the foolishness of yesterday has become
the wisdom of tomorrow."

—Sir William Osler, famed Canadian physician,
first chief of staff at Johns Hopkins Hospital

Even after starting my graduate studies in January 1972, I continued to clean houses part-time with Ben, keeping us in daily contact. I was taking my master's in sociology at St. John's University in the borough of Queens. While my classes in theory, research methods, and statistics were stimulating, my real intellectual curiosity still lay with what I had been witnessing as Ben's sidekick. Dissolving clouds and picking information out of the air indicated some underlying principle bigger than I could imagine. Before I had the chance to become bored by the repetitions, Ben had a breakthrough that set the future course of his life and a large chunk of mine.

We were in Ben's apartment with a few friends when one of them handed him a letter from a cousin in Dallas requesting a reading.

"Don't tell me any more," insisted Ben, taking the letter. "The less I know, the more specific I can be." After a few seconds, he grabbed his head. "I don't know what's going on, but I'm getting a headache like you wouldn't believe!" He put down the letter. The headache went away. He picked up the letter. The headache returned. He did this several more times.

"Maybe you shouldn't be touching the letter," I suggested.

"I'm going to make the pain go away!" he insisted.

Ben went into his bedroom, where he lay down holding the letter. About fifteen minutes later, he returned, completely exhausted but triumphant. "I made the pain go away!" he boasted.

Despite Ben's obvious satisfaction, it wasn't until the friend who had given Ben the letter phoned his cousin in Dallas to report on the reading that we discovered something genuinely new might have transpired. Apparently the Dallas cousin had been suffering a migraine while Ben had held the letter. When the pain left Ben's head, it had mysteriously left hers. Ben's intention had not been to cure her. All he had wanted to do was to rid himself of the excruciating pain in his own head.

During past readings, Ben had sometimes identified physical symptoms, but this was the first time he had experienced them in his own body. Once while holding the library card of a highly skeptical friend of mine, Ben placed his right hand just above his own lower back. "Your friend Doug has a back sprain about here. It's fairly recent. I think he hurt it lifting something. It's not serious now, but it could become chronic if he doesn't look after it. There's also tension in his shoulders, but that's just nerves." Ben then asked one of his rare questions: "What's your friend got to feel anxious about?"

"He's getting married."

"Tell him not to go through with it if he wants to get rid of the tension," advised Ben, who had a cynical view of that institution. Again his eyes glazed. "There's a lump behind your friend's left ear. Nothing serious though he's been concerned about it." He paused before adding, "I think it's a sebaceous cyst."

"What's that?"

"I have no idea. I just said it."

Since Ben never asked if he was right, I didn't tell him that a month earlier Doug had strained his back lifting a carton. Later, when I returned the library card, he also admitted to the tension in his shoulders. I myself saw the lump behind his left ear. A doctor would later diagnose it as a harmless sebaceous cyst.

Doug's reaction to Ben's diagnosis proved typical. While he was astounded by Ben's accuracy, he displayed no curiosity about the abilities of the man himself. The Doug Effect.

The Dallas letter marked the beginning of Ben's work as a diagnostician. As chance would have it, I became his first intentional cure.

We were in a client's kitchen taking a break from cleaning. Since the client had told Ben to help himself to anything he wanted, Ben was leaning against the refrigerator drinking coffee while I sat on a counter, legs dangling and nursing a glass of soda water. Since the Dallas-letter incident had happened the evening before, Ben was still a little wide-eyed about it: "I get this symptom like the top of my head has blown off. I imagine the pain is something I can dissolve, like clouds, and so I do it and I get better. Then I hear the woman with the migraine allegedly gets better about the same time. Am I making too much of this?"

I was glad to hear the word "allegedly." "You can't rule out coincidence," I responded sagely. "Pain comes and goes."

I should know. For about five years I had had such severe lower-back pain that I had to give up my swimming scholarship to Niagara University. After about one hundred yards of the butterfly, the stroke with which I had established a New York City record, I could no longer arch my back without debilitating pain. Now this pain had become chronic. I couldn't even stand too long without it kicking in. Assorted doctors had been unable to find anything structurally or neurologically wrong. Like so many others, I had no choice but to live with the condition while compensating with stretching exercises.

Feeling my back seize as we talked, I instinctively moved my chest closer to my knees, seeking relief. Ben had been leaning with his left shoulder against the refrigerator, gesturing easily with his right hand. Grimacing, he put down his coffee cup and placed his left hand on his lower spine. "My back hurts."

Keeping my voice casual, I asked, "Where?"

"Here. Under my hand. Boy, this is weird. It came on all of a sudden like with the letter." He began checking his pockets. "Maybe I'm carrying something from someone with a bad back." He opened his wallet. "I've got some checks from people, but I don't think that's it." He started to walk out of the kitchen, still favoring his back. "Maybe I've got something in my coat pocket."

"You dope!" I called after him. "Come back—it's me." Despite my discomfort, I felt pleased to have finally put something over on him. "And you call yourself a psychic!"

"Oh, great, now both of us have bad backs. Keep your pain to yourself!"

"Better yet, why don't you fix both of us?" I said.

"How?"

After sliding from the counter, I bent over the kitchen table. "Put your hand on my back."

"Why?"

"Just do it."

Ben put his left hand on the small of my back. Almost immediately it started to feel warm. Then hot. As the heat penetrated my spine, I felt my lower back grow numb in a four-inch radius, as if shot with Novocain. With Ben's hand still on my back, the numbness wore off from the outer edges in. When he removed his hand, the last spot of numbness disappeared. The entire experience had lasted less than ten minutes.

Ben announced, "My back doesn't hurt anymore."

Standing straight, I arched, gyrated, then touched my toes.

"What are you doing?" he asked.

"Trying to find the pain."

"Then it's gone, too?"

"Completely."

"You don't say!" mocked Ben, signaling the return of his trademark bravado. Typically, his ambivalence warred against his self-confessed megalomania until one or the other declared a temporary victory. At present his attitude telegraphed that, if anyone could heal, of course it would be him.

"What did you do this time?"

"Who knows? For the last few weeks I've had the feeling things were going to change without knowing how. When you asked for help, I had a hunch what was going to happen. As soon as I placed my hand on your back, I felt energy pulsing down my arm. It was automatic—the most natural thing in the world—and I knew this would be my next development."

"You're going to be a healer?" Though I was jumping with questions, the strange sadness in Ben's eyes made me realize that this was a moment best served by silence. Privately, I wondered how being able to heal could possibly be a cause for melancholy instead of excitement. As usual, Ben had sensed something I would have to learn the hard way. As he elaborated, "With this healing business, I'm opening up Pandora's box, and I'm not sure it's worth it. There's a big difference between giving out information and dealing with people's health. Imagine you can relieve pain, or heal, or whatever you want to call it. When people with terrible diseases seek you out, how are you going to ignore them? I'll end up spending the rest of my life being aggravated, when all I really want is to be left alone. The truth is, a lot of sick people don't really want to get better, despite what they say. They enjoy the attention their illness gives them, or maybe they just want an excuse to get out of their responsibilities. The people I treat successfully will resent me, the medical profession will scorn me, and I'll be regarded as a freak."

The way it turned out, Ben was accurate on all counts.

As for my back: though I imagined my relief might be temporary, the pain has never returned in thirty-five years. Despite participating in everything from athletic competitions, to lifting heavy furniture, I have never felt so much as a gnawing ache or a stab of pain. In fact, I would say my back is now exceptionally strong. If anyone wishes to argue that my symptoms must have been psychosomatic, that's fine with me. A cure is a cure is a cure.

Once Ben let it be known he would do healings, he had no shortage of clients. He began with minor problems for friends and neighbors, who told others, producing an inexhaustible supply. While dramatic one-shot cures such as mine were rare, a variety of conditions seemed to improve where there had been no improvement before.

Though I was fascinated with Ben's new career, these cases were relentlessly soft. Everything was mysterious. Nothing was controlled. It would have been convenient to accept these healings on faith, but I was stuck with being an empiricist. I needed to know how the treatment worked.

Grudgingly, Ben agreed once more to let me test his diagnostic work in a double-blind study, which I set up informally at Deepdale Hospital, in Little Neck, New York. As patients were admitted, they were asked voluntarily to sign an index card, which the admitting nurse then placed inside two opaque envelopes. We ended up with eight envelopes, and when I later handed each to Ben for a diagnosis, neither of us knew anything about the patient, not even their gender. He was right on all but one, and later we heard that Ben's diagnosis of that patient was confirmed when he or she was readmitted a month later because of the hospital's misdiagnosis.

Meanwhile, an event occurred that countered any lingering skepticism I might have had. Ben and I were with my sister, Lynn, and my girlfriend, who attempted to use a knife to pry off the tab on a can of soda.

"Be careful with that knife," Ben cautioned just as she stabbed her right forefinger, opening a deep wound. Leaping forward, Ben took her finger, now pouring blood, in his left hand.

"Stop squeezing," she protested. "It hurts."

But Ben wasn't squeezing. I could see space between his fingers and hers.

"Be quiet, it's healing," he insisted, refusing to let go.

Twenty minutes later, Ben did release my girlfriend's finger. Her wound had healed. No cut, no scar, no scab—no sign of injury beyond the spilt blood.

Different things impress different people. By then I'd had my back fixed and had witnessed many dramatic cures, but none affected me as profoundly as seeing my girlfriend's finger heal before my eyes. I was literally speechless while she, face ashen, kept picking at the place where her wound should have been, muttering, "Oh my God."

I think even Ben got scared, because he left almost immediately.

4. The Healings

"Miracles do not happen in contradiction to nature but only in contradiction to that which is known to us of nature."

—St. Augustine

It took about a year after I joined Ben as his cleaning partner for me to lose all his clients. By then he was working full-time as a healer. While he never charged for his readings, he did for his healings: pay what you want, if you want. At one point, I facetiously offered to make him a sign: SPECIAL OF THE DAY: LEUKEMIA $15. Many people paid him even less. He didn't seem to care, though his wife did.

People came in droves, from all walks of life and with every sort of complaint. There is, I discovered, a huge, loosely knit underground of desperate people in pain who have fallen through the cracks of the medical system. I also discovered that, despite Ben's continuous complaints about what was expected of him, he enjoyed being the center of attention. In fact, he was at his best when people needed him, and being a healer gave him a status more in keeping with what he felt was his true worth.

One of his early patients was a high school student named Mark, who arrived on crutches with his parents.

"I can't lift my right foot," he told Ben.

Though Ben didn't press for details, Mark's mother had a compulsion to supply them. Mark had been knocked unconscious for about five minutes during a football game a week earlier. When he came to, his foot was jerking uncontrollably. Suspecting neurological damage, doctors had prescribed the drug L-dopa for his Parkinson's-like symptoms. Though this relieved the spasms, Mark still couldn't move his ankle—a classic case of drop foot.

As I watched, Ben placed his chair opposite Mark so he could prop Mark's right foot on his own left knee. He passed his left hand repeatedly over Mark's ankle for about a minute, then announced, "I can't find anything wrong here. At least there's no pain."

"How do you know that?" demanded his father.

"If there was, I'd feel it."

Mark, an unusually shy person, remained silent.

Next Ben set Mark's foot on the floor and told him to move it. Though Mark could lift his whole leg, he had no mobility in his ankle. Now standing behind Mark, Ben placed his hands on Mark's shoulders near the neck in almost a stranglehold. After about five minutes, he passed his left hand over Mark's head, finally settling on the left side near the top. "The problem is here," he announced. "The injury is to your brain as your doctors said, not your ankle." Ben kept his hand there for more than fifteen minutes. "Okay, move your foot."

Using great concentration, Mark was able to raise his toes about three inches with his heel still touching the floor. Then with his toes on the floor, he raised his heel about two inches. Finally, with his foot flat, he rotated his ankle about an inch.

Mark beamed at his parents. "Look, it's moving!"

His father was dumbfounded, while his mother began to cry. I felt chills.

Ben removed his hands from Mark's shoulder. "That's enough for today. Come back tomorrow and we'll finish the job."

Mark was still beaming. "Thanks a lot, man. That was great!"

After the family left, Ben let me debrief him. "What just happened?" I asked.

"There's an energy that goes through me. I can feel it passing down my left arm and into my hand." He pointed to a spot on his left palm, slightly off center toward the thumb. "Here. I felt heat coming out that didn't seem to originate with me."

"What were you doing when you passed your hand over Mark's foot and head?"

"I was feeling for anything out of the ordinary, whatever that means. Since I didn't get anything over Mark's foot, on impulse I felt around his head, where I found a hot spot. I'm not sure if the heat was coming from his head or my hand or both, but it seemed natural to treat the hot spot."

"How come you were able to fix my back and my girl-friend's finger with one shot, but not Mark's foot?"

"The feeling in my hand began to diminish, and I got the impression that this was all the energy Mark could take. I'm quite sure his problem can be solved with more treatments."

And it was. After five more, Mark regained full use of his ankle.

Mark's case turned out to be the template. Ben would place his hands on a client's shoulders, or occasionally the solar plexus. After a few minutes, he would search for hot spots. Most often, but not always, they coincided with the area of complaint. Wherever they were, Ben concentrated on them.

Most treatments lasted from thirty to sixty minutes or more, depending on the severity of the condition. As Ben's popularity grew, his living room resembled a doctor's waiting room, except that this was where he worked, moving from person to person, treating as many as fifteen in one session.

I saw amazing things. At the risk of sounding biblical, I witnessed scenes in which the blind regained some vision, the deaf could once again hear, the lame could walk, along with a string of cancer cures that the medical profession summarily dismissed as spontaneous remissions. I never got over my wonder. While Ben's readings fascinated me, his healings riveted me.

Instantaneous cures of the sort I experienced were rare, though most treatments did produce noticeable effects. Sometimes they resulted in an initial worsening of symptoms, particularly with conditions involving pain. Though this alarmed me, Ben saw it as a necessary part of the larger healing process. Typically, people had to return several times for a complete cure, and sometimes even then it proved elusive. I remember Ben treating a forty-year-old woman week after week for severe rheumatoid arthritis, and though he relieved much of the pain and somewhat straightened her gnarled fingers, she was never cured.

Over the months I noted a relationship between the amount of time a condition had existed and the number of treatments needed to cure it. While someone recently blinded by an injury might regain sight relatively quickly, those blinded over the years from diabetes would experience only gradual restoration along with a reduction in their need for insulin. Conditions that might be described as natural were also difficult to change. For example, myopia, or nearsightedness, is not a disease of the eyeball but a problem resulting from its shape. When Ben treated me for that condition, my vision improved just enough so that my glasses caused strain. Since my eyes needed a lot more work, I found myself facing a prolonged period during which I would not be able to see with or without my glasses. Either that or I would have to be fitted with a new prescription after each treatment. Since neither prospect was practical, I opted to leave well enough alone, and my eyes readjusted to the old prescription.

My optical experience proved typical, causing Ben to muse about how much fun it would be to treat an optometrist with access to an unlimited gradation of lenses. Nevertheless, he elected to treat himself so that he was eventually able to discard his reading glasses.

None of this was faith healing, which by definition requires faith on the part of the healer, the patient, or both. Many people who had already visited faith healers would ask if they had to believe in anything special, to which Ben always said no. In fact it seemed to us that, all things being equal, the less people believed, the faster the healings happened, which is why we jokingly called Ben's practice "faithless healing." His favorite clients were those who started with the pronouncement, "I think this is a bunch of crap, but I have nowhere else to turn." Ben and I acknowledged from the get-go that as far as medical treatment was concerned, he was metaphorically at the bottom of the food chain.

A one-of-a-kind case centered on Nicholas, then in his twenties. All of his life he had wanted to be a state trooper, but the height requirement was 5 foot 8 and he was only 5 foot 7½. Ben and I treated him a few times, till one day he returned all excited. He was now a state trooper! Whether we gave him that extra half-inch or whether he managed to psych out the recruiting officer is something we'll never know.

Unlike most psychics, Ben never declared good days or bad. Successful healing depended on the problem under treatment, not on how he felt, and if he started in a grumpy mood, the work usually cheered him up. Similarly, he seemed oblivious to all distractions. He could heal one person while having a scrappy conversation with another. In fact, he claimed that this sort of peripheral emotional engagement improved his performance.

As he had discovered with the Dallas letter, Ben was also capable of long-distance healing, which we called "absent healing," but it drained him. When he put an item that belonged to a client under his pillow, he would awaken exhausted.

He also had unexpected failures. Someone being treated for a serious condition might announce, "Since I'm here anyway, would you treat this wart?" Ben couldn't cure warts or colds, though he might temporarily relieve congestion.

Ben produced spectacular results with a wide variety of cancers—so much so that his treatment, at the very least, could have served as a diagnostic tool. If a growth responded immediately, it was malignant. If it didn't, it was probably benign. Though the owner might object to it on aesthetic grounds, the body itself didn't seem to mind. His best prognosis for cure was an aggressive cancer in a youthful person who hadn't undergone radiation treatment or chemotherapy. By design, these are killers that destroy healthy cells as well as cancerous ones. Because the cancerous ones grow more rapidly than the healthy ones, the hope is that they will be affected sooner and therefore die off faster. Ben's treatment, by contrast, seemed to work by nurturing the healthy cells.

Ben hadn't gone very far into his healing practice before the strange psychological responses, which he had anticipated, began to pile up.

When seeking a cure, the first thing most people wanted to know up front was how long it would take. Many who entered the "hocus-pocus" world of hands-on healing seemed geared to expect instantaneous cures as validation, quite unlike the frustrations they were willing to endure within the traditional medical system. One man with leukemia was angry at Ben for not curing him in a single session. According to his logic, if Ben could drive his blood count up 40 percent in one week, then Ben should have been able to cure him on the spot rather than expecting him to come back.

To my everlasting astonishment, more than half of those who were not cured in one treatment never returned, even some who had experienced dramatic improvement with allergies, pain, and debilitating symptoms of cancer, diabetes, and arthritis. While this exasperated me, Ben was philosophical because he had predicted it. I had to conclude, as he had stated, that many people didn't want to get well. This was especially true of those who had been sick or in pain for a long time. They seemed to have grown dependent on their ailments as part of their identities. Life without illness was inconceivable to them, even as they went through the motions of desperately seeking relief, not only to satisfy those around them but to keep up the charade for themselves. Circulating among doctors, chiropractors, psychics, seers, healers, and the like had become an end in itself, not easily relinquished. The psychiatric literature is full of such cases, and no doubt many medical doctors suspect that a disconcertingly high proportion of their patients, for whom they dutifully write prescriptions, have emotional rather than physical problems.

I was especially taken by surprise when a very intelligent friend of mine demonstrated one of these aberrant responses. Walter was a fellow graduate student with whom I occasionally studied. One day while I was in the university library he appeared on crutches. About a week before he had experienced a sharp pain in his right leg that had steadily grown worse. Two doctors, a chiropractor, and a neurologist had not been able to help. As he spoke, his eyes welled and his teeth clenched. "It's very bad. Very, very bad. I'd like to take my leg off!"

Walter, who was from Nigeria, where men were supposed to be macho, was normally a master of under-statement. Now, when I told him about Ben, he backed away, almost tripping over his own crutches. "That's crazy."

I knew enough not to argue. "Okay, suit yourself." Walter was working on his third doctorate, and I thought *that* was crazy. "Enjoy the pain," I called cheerily as I walked off.

"Wait!" Walter hobbled after me. "Can your friend really help me?"

"What do you have to lose?"

I phoned Ben. Since he was in the middle of a healing session, he invited us to join in. The more details I gave Walter on the drive over, the unhappier he became.

Ben was treating a first-time patient for cancer when we arrived. Another woman was awaiting a third treat-ment on her rheumatoid arthritis—always a tough one for Ben. As soon as Ben finished with the cancer patient, he motioned for Walter to sit in the chair. After protesting that it wasn't his turn, Walter dutifully obeyed.

Ben followed his regular routine until his hands settled on a spot about three inches above Walter's knee. While everyone else in the room chatted, he treated Walter for about twenty minutes.

"How does your leg feel now?"

Blank faced, Walter replied, "I have no comment."

Unperturbed, Ben told him to wait while he treated the woman with arthritis.

I watched as Walter gingerly put pressure on his leg, then slowly walked back to his chair. Still avoiding my eyes, he massaged his leg, systematically lifting and lowering it.

After about five minutes, Ben told him, "If your leg still hurts, I'll treat it again. I never know how long it will take."

Walter repeated, "I have no comment."

"This isn't a press conference," I snapped. "How does your leg feel?"

Walter looked at me almost sorrowfully. Then at Ben. Then back at me. "I've been sitting here trying to make sense of what just happened. About five minutes after you put your hand on my leg, the pain went away." He added with embarrassment, "I've been trying to make the pain return."

Ben, who was still treating the arthritic woman, just nodded, but I was annoyed. "I think a little gratitude might be in order," I told Walter.

Ben gestured for me to calm down, while Walter walked normally around the room without his crutches. "I'm grateful, yes, but I'm also confused. I was raised in a tribal society that believes in magic and witch doctors, which I've rejected," Walter said.

"Walter thinks of himself as an intellectual," commented Ben. "He's a convert to the pursuit of the rational. Now I'm his tribal past that's haunting him."

Walter didn't say a word on the drive home. Every time I tried to strike up a conversation, he simply nodded. When

I dropped him off, he politely shook my hand. "Thank you. I appreciate all you've done."

We never studied together again. When we bumped into each other, he was friendly, but if I dared to ask about his leg, his face would go blank: the Walter Effect.

Later, when I discussed Walter's case with Ben, he replied, "If you understand Walter's problem with hands-on healing, you'll understand why the scientific and medical communities will never go for it either."

I didn't believe him. Why would professionals, devoted to easing the suffering of their patients, reject a method so effective, so inexpensive, and so free of damaging side effects?

That was something else I had to learn, and unfortunately I would soon have plenty of opportunity. In case after case, I observed physicians dismiss Ben's cures, backed up by their own X-rays, CAT scans, or blood tests, as "just" spontaneous remission. No one wanted to follow up. No one wanted to see if more than coincidence was involved. No one was interested in the overall pattern, which we were witnessing on a daily basis. While it's certainly true that cancers do remit, a single doctor is lucky to see one of these cases in his career, much less dozens in a row. If Ben had been curing only one particular type of cancer, we could at least have calculated the odds against remission, but he was banishing all kinds. His spectacular success was the toughest evidence against him.

Take the case of Nancy, who had an operation scheduled to remove a gangrenous foot. Two days after seeing Ben, the gangrene was gone. Her doctor was deeply shaken. Gangrene doesn't remit, and when Nancy asked if he would like to meet the man who cured her, he declined: "If I accept this, I'd have to throw out my medical training. What I've seen here is impossible." Unlike most doctors, he was generous enough to add, "I don't want to meet your healer, but off the record, I recommend you see him rather than me."

In at least one case, a doctor's "too good to be true" dismissal proved tragic. Lillian was an operating-room nurse whom I met through one of her co-workers. Though her sort of duties sometimes make people hard-edged and cynical, Lillian was exceptionally nice, quiet, and compassionate. She cared.

Three years previously, Lillian had precancerous lesions removed from her breast without complications. Now an exploratory operation revealed that cancer had invaded her body with a vengeance—it was everywhere. She had difficulty breathing, possessed no appetite, and tired easily. Her prognosis was several months at best.

At my friend's request, I put Lillian in touch with Ben. Though my friend was skeptical about Ben's lack of formal documentation, he was desperate on Lillian's behalf. She was only twenty-two.

While Lillian seemed composed, her husband, Tony, was frantic enough for both of them. He kept repeating, "I thought this was all over. It's a nightmare."

Ben canceled his appointments for the day so he could concentrate on Lillian.

"My cancer has metastasized into all my major organs," she told him in a straightforward, clinical manner. "I have an appointment with an oncologist in two days, but both my surgeon and internist have pretty much told me there's not a lot of hope."

Ben just nodded. "Let's see what we can do."

He treated her for two hours straight, after which she seemed to be breathing much easier. On her way out, I overheard her tell Tony that she was hungry.

When Lillian returned the next day, we saw a dramatic change. Instead of huffing and puffing, she walked with a spring to her step. After Ben treated her for another two hours, she was laughing and joking about silly things.

On her third day, Lillian arrived in a state of excitement. "Tony and I went bowling last night," she told us. "I feel like a new person."

Even Tony felt relaxed enough to kid her, "She still can't bowl!"

After Ben treated Lillian for another hour, she left for her medical appointment.

Ben seemed pleased with himself. "I've never treated anyone so intensely," he confided. "Something has happened to Lillian. I can feel it."

Indeed it had. I was still with Ben when Lillian phoned several hours later. While I waited in the living room, he talked privately with her for a long time before slumping in a chair beside me. He looked beaten. "They can't find any cancer," he announced.

I let out a whoop, to which Ben didn't respond. "Am I missing something?"

According to Lillian, when her radiologist examined her with X-rays and CAT scans to see how far her masses had progressed, he found no tumors at all. He checked her with a different machine. Same results. A blood sample supported these findings—no cancer. In her excitement, Lillian told him about Ben's treatment. The doctor dismissed her account as being without value, then insisted instead on proceeding with the rule-book treatment for her condition.

"What condition?" I demanded.

"The one she used to have, which the doctor assumes she must still have. They don't believe the tests. Or maybe it's supposed to be preventative—some protocol the medical profession is expected to follow."

"What does Lillian say?"

"She told me she was grateful to me, but she'd decided to go through with the treatments just to be on the safe side. I couldn't talk her out of it."

"What's the worst that could happen?"

"That stuff is lethal!" exclaimed Ben.

Lillian was given radiation at the uppermost limits, combined with massive dosages of chemotherapy. Since her original diagnosis indicated she had little hope, her doctors thought it worth giving her this outside chance.

Throughout, Lillian behaved like an obedient nurse. She accepted whatever the doctors ordered. Her hair fell out and she took on the sick, bloated look of a chemotherapy patient. Though Ben went to the hospital to try to counter the aftereffects of the treatments, he was no match for the damage. Since Lillian's lungs had received so much radiation, one stopped functioning and was surgically removed. Several hours after the operation, Lillian died of heart failure. Mercifully, the staff made no serious attempt to revive her.

As a matter of routine, Lillian's lung was sent to the pathology department for postmortem analysis. Off the record, we learned that the report was negative for cancer.

Of all our cases, Lillian's was the one that affected both Ben and me most deeply. Though Ben was always exasperated when his clients accepted their physicians' explanation of spontaneous remission, never before had this knee-jerk medical dismissal produced such crushing results. Lillian's death filled him with such outrage, he might have retired if it weren't for the responsibility he felt toward others still in treatment. He settled instead for drastically changing the way he practiced.

5. The Sorcerer's Apprentice

*"Science today is locked into paradigms. Every avenue is blocked by
beliefs that are wrong, and if you try to get anything published by a
journal today, you will run against a paradigm and the editors will
turn it down."*

—SIR FRED HOYLE, astronomer

FOR AS LONG AS I HAD KNOWN BEN, he had been a quirky character with a pessimistic view of life. Now his healing work, with
its whirlwind of triumphs and tragedies, was pushing him further into dark territory. Because he couldn't always separate
his inner and outer worlds, he couldn't always distinguish
between what someone said and what that person thought.
This caused him to utter confusing comments in reply to
statements that no one had made.

One of our strangest arguments—close to a screaming
match—occurred when Ben accused me, in front of wit-
nesses, of interrupting him when I had just been sitting
quietly watching him work. If we were in different rooms,
it was even harder for him to separate spoken words from
unspoken thoughts.

Ben sometimes joked that he didn't really belong on this planet. He said that he was from the Alpha Centauri star system (a favorite of sci-fi buffs) and that I was his astral twin. Like most successful humor, it reflected an underlying truth—how alien he felt in a world he didn't understand. Most of us have strong filters—some natural, some culturally inspired—making us oblivious to 99.99 percent of what's going on around us, but Ben's boundaries were crumbling. He was being flooded with sensations he couldn't always sort out. It was a very dangerous place for him, and more than once he talked of suicide.

In an attempt to heal the healer, I took Ben to see a psychiatrist with an office in Manhattan. After a private assessment, she invited Ben to participate in a group session. Since I wasn't present, the rest of this story is his. It sounds accurate to me.

The psychiatrist's patients were sitting in a circle discussing their problems, as many had been doing for years. When Ben didn't contribute, the psychiatrist prompted him, and of course it was like uncorking a bottle and releasing the genie. Ben went around the circle, telling each patient the source of his or her problem in stunning detail. "You suffered this trauma on this date, and you wrote about it in this letter that's sitting in your left-hand dresser drawer behind the socks." One old guy was so moved he broke down in tears. The group turned to Ben, and naturally the psychiatrist felt professionally threatened. I suppose she was still in shock when she informed him on his way out, "Based on your symptoms, I would diagnose you as a minimal paranoid schizophrenic. Trouble is, when you say you see and hear things, you clearly do, and when you think people are rejecting you, that's right, too."

She then proved the truth of that last statement by terminating Ben's therapy. As far as Ben was concerned, this was yet another example of my dragging him to "experts" who were anything but.

Although my relationship with Ben had remained surprisingly constant, my life was changing in almost every other way. In April 1973 I married, and in December of that same year I graduated from St. John's University with my MA in sociology. I was now teaching a variety of sociology courses at City University of New York and Elizabeth Seton College in Westchester County, which is part of New York's metropolitan area. Then, in March 1975, my father, Earl, died suddenly at age fifty-seven. That was a death I had spookily predicted several years before.

At age nineteen, I had awakened from a vivid dream in which I had witnessed my father having a massive heart attack. When my mother phoned that morning to report what I already knew, I heard myself blurting out that he would be fine this time, but that he would have a second, fatal attack in several years. That insight came to me just the way Ben described information coming to him. In 1975, right on schedule, that's what happened. Since Pa was overweight, a smoker, and a heavy drinker even after his first heart attack, you could discount my prediction as merely describing a predictable quasi suicide; however, this was one of several deaths that I had dreamed about in advance as a teenager. Those dreams, which were always very dramatic and qualitatively different from other dreams, always bothered me because I didn't know what to do with them. Someone whom I didn't know well, or hadn't seen for a while, would come into my thoughts, and I wouldn't be able to banish them. Next, I would have a dream about some kind of accident, which would then happen to that person, and they would end up dead.

I remember Charlie, a fellow in my neighborhood, who was killed in a car crash at age sixteen. Though two others died with him, his image was the only one that had gnawed at my brain. I also dreamed about another Charlie, the brother of my closest childhood friend, overdosing on drugs, which is exactly what he did, probably because they were illegal and he didn't know the dosage. Once again, you could look back and say he was a person at risk, and anyone could predict that. Also, since more deaths occurred than I foresaw in prophetic dreams, this wasn't a high-performance thing with me. If you read the ESP literature, both scholarly and popular, you'll find that prophetic dreams abound. I don't know if my experiences were unusual, or if I had just escaped the cultural bias that encourages us to deny psychic events.

These youthful dreams of doom left me with a sense of wonder and curiosity, inspiring me to read books on the paranormal, at first haphazardly. In Ruth Montgomery's *Search for the Truth*,[1] she wrote about receiving spirit messages through automatic writing. That sounded cool, but when I sat with a pen, emptying my mind to hear from the Great Beyond, nothing ever happened. Same with Ouija boards. With *my* fingers on a planchette, it never, ever moved. As far as I was concerned, the jury deciding whether I possessed psychic ability was still out. Nevertheless, about a year into Ben's healing practice, I began working alongside him just as I had done with the cleaning. He said that the healings went faster that way, and the difference was qualitative, not just quantitative. He also claimed that I had the ability to heal on my own if I chose.

"You've spent so much time with me that some of my stuff has rubbed off on you," he said, "but I think you could do it anyway. I can feel it. I draw upon your energy the same as I do on my own."

Though it was fun to partner with Ben, I was glad to avoid full responsibility. Like a student who has apprenticed with Picasso, I was reluctant to set up my own easel and start drawing stick figures. Eventually I did go solo—nothing big at first, just aches and pains, with which I seemed successful. I also discovered that my sensations as a healer echoed Ben's. I, too, experienced a surge of energy and the heating-up of my hands. I, too, felt hot spots, sometimes in the afflicted area, sometimes in another part of a client's body. Before this I had wrongly assumed that it was Ben who had produced the hot spots, which anyone else could then feel.

Along with this clinical work, I also studied the literature on energy healing.

I discovered that in most societies except ours, the preferred medical model has been holistic. Both tribal and Eastern healers traditionally diagnose disease as an imbalance in a person's mind/body/spirit, or in that person's relationship to his or her society and environment.

In Chinese acupuncture, needles are inserted at specific points in the body to unblock the flow of *chi*, defined as an invisible universal energy, which is thought to be the key to all healing: physical, spiritual, and emotional. Indian yoga is a system of physical and breathing exercises, designed to activate the *chakras*, or energy centers, for the release of *kundalini* or *prana*. This is also described as a universal energy, or life-force, believed to increase physical and mental well-being, and to lead to spiritual enlightenment. Similarly, shamanic rituals—utilizing dancing, drumming, chanting, and sweating—also release energies that are said to activate the immune system and open the world of spirit.

Even Western medicine is rooted in holistic belief. The English word "health" derives from the archaic word "hale," meaning "whole." So does the word "holy." By contrast, today's medical practitioners place their faith in technology, surgery, and antiviral warfare, with areas of expertise divided into ever-more-discrete specialties. Given the many wonders this approach has produced, it's perhaps not surprising that our medical establishment regards hands-on healing with great skepticism, if not outright distaste. This attitude persists despite the fact that many patients are opting, with accelerating enthusiasm, for complementary and alternative medicine.

Back in the seventies when I was working with Ben, this intercultural bridge had not yet been constructed. What did exist was a small but compelling core of laboratory evidence supporting mind-body healing. I was especially impressed by the findings of Bernard Grad, a research oncologist on the faculty of McGill University, in Montreal. During the sixties and seventies, Grad extensively tested Oskar Estebany, an uneducated Hungarian who reputedly cured through the laying-on of hands. Estebany had discovered his talent while in the Hungarian cavalry when sick horses he petted mysteriously revived. He made no outlandish claims for himself; in fact, he couldn't understand what all the fuss was about, because he wasn't consciously doing anything that didn't come naturally. He had no faith, did not go into a trance, and he eschewed all showbiz gimmicks. Still, people kept insisting Estebany's hands produced remarkable cures, and after many years of this, he volunteered to be scientifically tested. Refreshingly, he himself had remained a skeptic.

In one experiment, Grad divided a batch of surgically wounded mice into two groups: one to be treated and one as a control. Those whose cage Estebany held for fifteen minutes twice daily healed significantly more rapidly than the untreated control group.[2]

In another experiment, Grad divided mice with induced goiters into three groups. Estebany was to hold the first cage of mice twice daily for fifteen minutes, five days a week over a period of forty days; the second was to be treated with the heat equivalent of being touched; the third was to be left untreated. Although all the mice developed goiters, those handled by Estebany did so at a significantly slower rate.

To see if Estebany's hands emitted a force that could charge other substances, Grad exposed some mice to scraps of cotton and wool that Estebany had treated, while a control group was exposed to untouched scraps. Again, mice in contact with the treated scraps showed a significantly slower rate of goiter formation, implying that Estebany's hands had transmitted energy.[3]

In another set of experiments, the biochemist Dr. Justa Smith of Rosary Hill College, in Buffalo, instructed Estebany to hold a test tube containing a solution of the digestive enzyme trypsin. She was attempting to see if Estebany healed by speeding up the catalyzing activity of these naturally occurring proteins. The longer Estebany held the test tube, the faster the enzyme trypsin catalyzed; however, when Estebany held other enzymes, Smith found their reaction rate decreased. By employing different psychic healers, she confirmed these findings. Some enzymes always accelerated while others always slowed. This perplexing result made no sense until Smith realized a unifying factor: the direction of enzyme activity always corresponded to the greater health of the organism.[4]

In studies by Dr. Dolores Krieger of New York University, the blood of sick people who Estebany treated by the laying-on of hands showed a significant increase in hemoglobin when compared with the blood of patients in a control group, suggesting an immune response. This was true even of cancer patients simultaneously treated with drugs known to induce anemia. More striking was the improvement or disappearance of brain tumors and other gross symptoms of emphysema, rheumatoid arthritis, and other common conditions.[5]

All these experiments proceeded along traditional scientific lines despite their unorthodox premises: an attempt was being made to explain the mysterious in terms of ordinary cause and effect.

I liked those experiments. I liked them a great deal. They were real science with hard empirical results that had direct application outside the lab, created by researchers who followed the accepted protocols. Many years later, I would have an opportunity to meet and know the Great Grad who pioneered these experiments, and I would not be disappointed.

I would also have repeated opportunities to verify an observation I had already made: how little impact Grad's astonishing findings seemed to make on the scientific community. When he or his researchers would present them at biological conventions, the audience seldom reacted. No one disputed his methods or his conclusions. Instead, both skeptics and those interested in alternative healing remained strangely silent. Even in the literature on healing, I found only passing references to Grad's experiments, with few attempts to replicate them.

Despite these red flags, the empiricist in me wanted to push into the territory Grad had opened. I knew from all I had witnessed that Ben had the problem of reliability beaten. I yearned to carry out research that would prove beyond all doubt that his hands-on treatments produced verifiable results, and I was still naive enough to imagine it would matter.

There was another red flag that I missed. Ben and I were approaching a crossroads where he would need to take one path while I would need to take a different one.

Our parting would not be amicable.

6. Crossroads

*"The voyage of discovery lies not in seeking new horizons,
but in seeing with new eyes."*

—Marcel Proust

Because of Lillian's horrific death, Ben introduced changes designed to formalize his practice. The first one, which I suggested, was to require all new clients to provide at least verbal assurances that their doctors had knowledge of his treatments. If anyone balked, Ben insisted that they either find a new doctor or a new healer. Ben's second innovation was to require his clients to take a more active role in their own healing. This meant teaching them his method so they could practice along with him.

Like many other healers, Ben believed that disease could be diagnosed through "tuning in" to a body's energies. He also believed that he himself healed through the transmission of some sort of energy that created the sensation of heat as it passed through his hands. Some healers feel they are conduits for divine power; some claim to work through spirit guides; some take personal credit; some feel they merely tap into abilities all of us possess. Some heal by placing their hands on their patients; some manipulate energy surrounding the body; some believe they can treat at a distance. Ben's technique differed from so many others in his attitude toward the role of the mind, or consciousness. Most alternative healers stress the need for positive thinking, both by themselves and by their patients. For instance, if dealing with a brain tumor, the healer and patient might intently visualize a healthy brain without the tumor, perhaps simultaneously calling on a higher power. By contrast, Ben healed through detachment—distracting his mind from his hands in order to let them move unimpeded by intellect or ego. Typically he would carry on all manner of unrelated conversations while treating a patient, because he said the treatment worked better that way.

Ben's reason for distracting his mind derived from his belief that he was not the origin of the healing power that cured his patients. That came from a place he could experience but not define—a place I later would call the "Source." Unlike healers who consider themselves the channel of divine power, Ben refused to connect this energy with any kind of faith or religious belief. The process of connection was a natural one that conscious thought impeded.

If Ben's patients were to become active but detached participants, we had to figure out how to distract them from focusing on the afflictions they so desperately wanted cured. Ben's technique emerged out of his own instinct, while my job was the pragmatic one—to analyze what he was doing as best I could in order to try to replicate it. Neither one of us knew what "it" was, how it worked, or why.

Together Ben and I devised a two-step method for diverting his patient's minds with mental images that had no direct connection to healing. Summarized, the rules for Step One go like this (for a fuller guide to this technique, turn to page 224 in Appendix A):

1. Make a list of at least twenty things that you don't have and would like—objects, honors, physical or psychological desires.

2. Translate each item into a visual image suggesting the wish has already been granted. For example, don't think about the bad knee you want to heal. Instead imagine yourself playing tennis or doing something else you could only do if your knee were healed.

3. Choose images that are ends and not means. Don't imagine yourself with a pile of money. Instead, visualize the red Jaguar you'd buy if you had the money. Don't think about how that might happen—just seize on the image as if it were already a reality.

4. Make every image personal to yourself and completely selfish. Forget about world peace and child poverty. This isn't the place for altruism or abstracts.

5. Don't include anyone else on your list without his or her permission. Don't, for example, try to imagine a friend cured of arthritis without that person's agreement. Humans are infinitely complex creatures, and what may seem obvious to you may prove anything but. The one exception involves those unable to give permission, such as small children, people in a coma, or animals.

6. Once the list has been compiled, regard every item on it as equal. The desire for a new computer is therefore no more important than imagining yourself winning an international golf tournament.

Step Two—the application of the list—is something I call cycling (again, please turn to page 230 in Appendix A for a fuller explanation of this technique and the rationale behind it):

1. Memorize the list by visualizing each image, one item after another, for about a second.

2. Practice until the list is so well memorized that you can run it in any order—backward, forward, at random.

3. Run the list through your mind whenever you're experiencing an emotion. It doesn't matter whether it's love or rage. Positive and negative feelings are the same for this purpose, and the stronger the better.

4. Next, speed up the process by flipping through the images until they become a blur. At first this may require great effort, but the more you practice, the more natural it becomes.

5. You'll know you have mastered the technique when you find yourself automatically cycling while experiencing an emotion without having to prompt yourself.

When Ben tried to teach cycling to each new patient, it sounded so counterintuitive to him that he found himself tortured by the sheer repetitiveness of the questions he was required to answer. His solution was to create biweekly training forums, which anyone wanting treatment was required to attend.

About ten people came to his first meeting—the only ones left in his practice after he had imposed his new conditions. Though our mental-imaging technique had seemed simple to us, once again Ben had trouble convincing the group that what they were practicing could have anything to do with healing. After the group overcame its initial resistance, he demonstrated his physical procedure:

"Place your hands on your patient's shoulders, then imagine an energy flowing down your arms. Don't concentrate. Just let it happen. It's important not to try to heal. Let the energy do that by itself. After you've started the process, go into the mental-imaging technique."

And so it went, week after week, with members of the group practicing on each other and then being encouraged by Ben to treat outsiders. Soon testimonials were a routine part of the meetings. Each member was expected to report on whom he or she had treated that week and what had been achieved. No matter how fantastic the claim, Ben would nod knowingly. "Anything I can do, you can do. And more."

Perhaps out of boredom, he began embellishing the benefits of the technique. As well as enhancing hands-on healing, it would reduce stress, leading to physiological changes promising greater longevity. The same technique could also be used for wish-fulfillment in every other aspect of life.

When I first heard Ben advertise these new claims, I became excited all over again. Time after time I had watched him perform healings that the medical profession declared impossible. Could he be right about these new claims? As usual, I began designing tests to measure his expanded list of advantages. As usual, Ben resisted. "We went the testing route once before. That's enough. I don't need it and neither do you."

But I did need it. My drive to push beyond case studies and anecdotes into hard, replicable science had moved into high gear.

Meanwhile, the group was taking on a life of its own. Mesmerized by Ben's new promises, those under treatment asked if they could bring friends. They in turn brought others. Finally, those with ailments were in the minority. Now Ben had an audience and, like any performer, he felt obliged to supply a show. This he did with gusto.

I was becoming alarmed. Although average attendance had increased to about twenty-five, Ben seemed to be doing less healing of his own. When members drifted away, Ben attributed it to some character defect. If I raised concerns, he adopted a contradictory stance: "I'm trying to get them not to need me anymore. They can do it for themselves, just as you can." Even Ben's wife seemed happy because he had agreed to charge a few dollars per person per meeting, which was now his chief source of income.

In the past, Ben had relished my questions. Now any challenges were increasingly interpreted as a lack of faith—the requirement we had always avoided. "If the meetings bother you, then you don't have to attend," he finally exclaimed in a pique.

Despite—or because of—my concerns, I couldn't stay away. Over the next few months I watched the group change again. Once its members had grown accustomed to healing, they wanted more, so Ben taught them how to do readings. "Hold an object in your left palm, clear your mind, then say the first thing that comes to you. Don't intellectualize what you feel. Just speak when you have the urge."

Though members of the group saw this as something new, I saw it as a regression, and while some seemed quite good at it, no attempt was made to screen for sensory cues or to establish other controls. When I pointed this out to Ben, his resentment flared into anger. "This isn't one of your damned parapsychology tests! This is the real thing. Don't you think I can tell if someone can do a reading or not?"

Increasingly, I found myself in a curious position at the meetings. Because I'd known Ben the longest, Ben and the others encouraged me to provide personal testimony. "Let Bill tell you about the time that . . ."

In the beginning, I confess that I enjoyed my enhanced status as "first among equals." Later it grew tiresome, then unnerving, as I found myself making halfhearted efforts to defend Ben against my own criticism. He was beginning to live in the past, and I was the stooge he counted on to prop him up.

One positive and far-reaching result of Ben's group was the opportunity to meet David Krinsley, a geology professor from Queens College of the City University of New York, who was then in his mid-forties. Dave's specialty was electron microscopy—the study of very, very small things. As well as working on the moon rocks and as a NASA consultant, he was a fellow of King's College of Cambridge University and the author of hundreds of scientific papers, including cover articles for the prestigious *Science* and *Nature* magazines.

Dave first attended the groups with a friend whom Ben was treating for diabetes. As I would learn, Dave had a long-time interest in paranormal phenomena that he referred to as "ESP stuff." He also shared my frustration about the lack of scientific rigor in much of the field. Both of us wanted Ben to progress from the clinical model, featuring people with their complexity of problems, to the experimental model, utilizing animals whose genetics and environment could be controlled. Our mutual desire was to design an unambiguous test that would have no viable counterhypothesis: a success that would prove the method, case closed.

As well as possessing an outstanding reputation in his own field, Dave had served as an interim provost at Queens College of the City University of New York, giving him a broad-based knowledge of other faculties. If we could design the right experiment, he believed he could persuade the chairman of the Queens biology department to help us conduct it. Though the biology chair thought hands-on healing was a joke, Dave's persistence persuaded the chair to cooperate, albeit unenthusiastically. Since the chairman was a fruit-fly specialist, we tossed around ideas focused on these lab favorites. What would happen if we treated a bunch of fruit flies? Would we be looking for genetic mutations?

Fortunately, a researcher in the biology department had been experimenting for about twenty years on mice injected with mammary cancer. Since Ben's most dramatic cures had been with cancer, this was ideal for us, and she was assigned to oversee our experiment. The type of mice she would be using were a standard, off-the-shelf model, well-defined through many generations and a multitude of other experiments. While I didn't relish animal testing, I knew it was essential for controlled studies. We would know at the outset the mice's expected life span, their diet, their habitual exposure to light, and how they typically responded to cancer injections.

Our most pressing problem was how to get Ben on board. His biweekly forums had by now morphed into rambling lectures on what he called "universal energy channeled by the superconscious mind." After listening in rapt attention, the members would hold discussions seasoned with quotes from the Kabbalah, the *Tibetan Book of the Dead,* the Koran, the Bible, astrology, numerology, and a host of other "ologies." No matter how learned these conversations might or might not be, they had nothing to do with anything that could be proven.

Landing Ben wasn't easy; however, by challenging him in front of his audience, and by playing on his resentment over his rejection by the medical community, Dave and I managed to get him to commit to the lab experiments.

Everything seemed ready for liftoff. The mice were expected in two weeks. The biology associate (whose name, because of protocol, I would never know) would inject all twelve mice with mammary cancer (adenocarcinoma, code H2712; host strain C3H/HeJ; strain of origin C3H/HeHu). Three days later, six would be given to Ben to be treated on a daily basis, while the other six would remain with the associate as a control group. According to the extensive scientific literature, injecting mice with this lethal strain resulted in 100 percent fatality between fourteen to twenty-seven days.[1]

The mice did not arrive on schedule. We were told it would require another week. That shipment did not arrive either. We had a third cancellation. When the mice finally did appear, my relief was short-lived. By then we'd lost our healer. According to Ben, the repeated failure of the mice to arrive was a sign—from wherever signs emanate—that he should not, would not, must not participate in the mice experiments. He had other plans that did not include time wasted in laboratories. Because he already knew that the more he and his followers achieved, the more the world would reject them, so had he decided to establish his own teaching, learning, and healing center. Specifically, he was going to become a minister of the Universal Life Church as a prelude to creating his own community. Founded in 1959, the ULC today claims twenty million ordained ministers. You can even download a form offering instant, no-fee ordination.

I couldn't believe what I was hearing. "You mean you're going to convert to some religion?" I asked Ben.

"Not in the traditional sense. If I form a religious community, everyone will leave us alone and we'll get tax advantages. That's where you come in. I want you to be an officer."

I was flabbergasted. Ben had always insisted that religion propagated more suffering than just about anything else. Now he assured me, "This is the answer I've been looking for. We'll finally be able to do our own thing."

I felt sorry for Ben. He seemed to be losing it. I felt sorry for myself. For four years he had been a friend and mentor who had helped define my life. I used to feel good in his presence. Now my stomach often knotted. I also felt sorry for the sick people who would suffer because of this lost opportunity to validate hands-on healing.

Dave refused to join in this lament. He wanted to go ahead with the experiment. He had a solution to Ben's abdication—Plan B. I would substitute for Ben.

Since Dave loved gadgets, he invited me to his geology lab, where he had tools for testing psychic abilities. We began with a specially weighted compass with a needle, which Russian psychics were reputedly able to mentally deflect.

First I tried concentration, urging it to move, then I tried not concentrating on it while passing my hands over it with detachment. Nothing happened—just like with automatic writing and the Ouija board planchette. Dave said he thought he saw a slight movement, but that was probably wishful thinking.

My next test was to read an unfamiliar object—something I had tried a couple of times in Ben's groups with limited success. After pouring sand from a test tube on my hand, Dave suggested cheerfully, "See what you get from this."

Mimicking Ben, I held the sand in my left palm, allowing my mind to go blank. As a former lifeguard, I associated sand with warm weather and beaches; however, after about two minutes of self-conscious silence, a glacier suddenly appeared in my mind's eye. No matter how hard I tried to erase this unlikely image, it grew sharper and more detailed.

Apologetically, I announced, "I see a glacier. Really, it's the edge of a glacier with a bunch of trees to the left growing right up to the ice."

Dave was visibly excited. "That's remarkable! It wasn't sand I gave you. It's a special kind of silt found only at the edge of glaciers. The scene you described exactly fits the location where this sample was taken."

During the next couple of days, I secretly kept hoping Ben would call so we could patch up our differences. Of course, I could have phoned him, but I wasn't into blind

faith or revealed truth as he now required. Our last conversation had merely formalized a split that had already
occurred. I felt hurt and bewildered that our relationship
had turned so toxic. I also knew that even if Ben and I
salvaged our relationship, I would never entice him into
the laboratory.

Usually I fall asleep in ten minutes—before exams, in
thunderstorms, it doesn't matter. However, the night
before I was to receive my mice, I had a rare bout of
insomnia. What exactly were my qualifications as a healer?
What if I succeeded? What if I failed? Both possibilities
seemed equally daunting.

7. Of Mice and Men

*"The beginning of knowledge is the discovery of something
we do not understand."*

—FRANK HERBERT, science-fiction writer

WHEN I PICKED UP MY INJECTED MICE, I tried to appear
excited. To create this opportunity, for which I had pushed
so hard, Dave had called in favors and was also sharing
costs. Though these were modest, this was yet another factor demonstrating his commitment.

Now that I was the guinea-pig healer, my arm's-length
distance from the planning process worked in favor of protocol. I had never met the chair of the biology department,
and I would be treating the mice in a small storeroom
away from the lab, where I could come and go as I pleased.
I would never see the control mice, which were now in the
possession of the associate biologist.

Because Ben usually treated clients for thirty to sixty
minutes once or twice a week, I decided I should treat my

mice daily for a full hour. On day 1, I spent at least twenty minutes rearranging the items stored helter-skelter in the storeroom, rather like a prisoner personalizing his cell for the long haul. When I ran out of ways to procrastinate, I gingerly picked up the cage to examine my patients for the first time. Instead of six mice, there were only five, one having already died of natural causes. They were brown, not white, as my layman's version of laboratory experiments had assumed. The transparent plastic cage was standard issue—about fourteen inches long by eight inches wide by five inches high, with a punctured metal top. At one end was a water bottle and a continuous feeder filled with smelly brown pellets.

Dave and I had agreed that I would not touch the mice. Instead, I would treat the cage containing them. In that way, all would be treated equally. Now with my hands on either side, I followed the routine I had practiced so many times with Ben, imagining an energy flowing down my left arm, out my hand, through the cage, and into the mice, then out the other side into my right hand and up my arm. I was aiming for "concentrated detachment"—not trying to heal, just allowing it to happen, carrying in my mind the desired intent for that outcome while not consciously concerning myself about how it might occur.

I waited expectantly to feel heat or a tingling in my left hand. Nothing. After about five minutes I found myself panicking, like an athlete whose muscles seize up on the day of the big race. I kept checking my watch—only one minute? It felt like ten. All confidence in myself and in the process evaporated. Belatedly I remembered to apply the mental-imaging technique Ben and I had designed. Though I'm not sure that adding this had any effect on the mice, it did wonders for me. At last I felt my left hand heat up, then the beginning of a current passing through me and, presumably, the mice. I stopped mental imaging and simply let the energy flow.

That first session established the pattern for those that followed. Usually my left hand would heat up for the duration. If it cooled after about twenty minutes, I still kept my palms against the cage for the entire hour. The more confident I felt, the more detached I became. My hands seemed to be working automatically while I observed.

Along with the desired detachment came intense boredom. Sometimes I would prop open a book or bring a radio, though I never lost my awareness of the mice. I could now empathize with what Ben must have gone through during his years of healing. At least with people there could be dialogue. Ironically, Ben probably would have preferred the mice.

On rare occasions, an indescribable feeling overcame me. I would be watching the mice or reading, when suddenly my whole body felt bathed in a warm glow. The detachment I felt from my hands, then my entire body, coalesced into a sense of oneness with the mice. All my doubts about the healings seemed trivial, and I was pervaded with peace and well-being. My mind emptied of thought. I simply was.

These sensations probably lasted about one to two minutes, leaving me relaxed and happy. I was never consciously able to create the experience. It happened or it didn't—a gift of grace.

About a week into the treatment, I was changing the litter in the cage when I observed lumps on two of the mice. One had a growth near its left hind leg, while the other had one near its left front leg. Since Dave and I had anticipated that a successful treatment meant no cancer would occur, this was very depressing. And it got worse. Two more mice developed lumps, while those on the first two continued to grow bigger. When all five had tumors, I called Dave, ready to end the obviously failed experiment by putting the mice out of their misery. He urged me to continue until he had a chance to come to the storeroom and see for himself.

To say I now harbored doubts would be a gross understatement. By the time Dave arrived, all the mice were misshapen with tumors. One had a third of its leg consumed by a growth. I was devastated.

Before his visit, Dave had consulted with our biologist. He repeated to me what she told him: "This is a cancer that doesn't spread. Instead, the mice get large external tumors that press against their internal organs, depriving them of nutrients and causing death through malnutrition."

Now I felt worse. "These mice are obviously dying."

Dave wasn't convinced. "They're acting quite normally."

It was true. Even the mouse with the largest tumor continued to scuttle around the cage, occasionally fighting with the others. I had tried to calm them down, afraid they might injure one another—unconsciously, I suppose, I wanted sick mice to act like sick mice. I also noticed that when I picked up the cage to begin a treatment, the mice would gravitate to my left palm, even laying their tumors against it. When I turned the cage so my left palm was on the other side, the mice shifted too.

During the next few days, Dave pressured me into keeping the experiment going. Odd blackened spots like pencil points had appeared on some, then all, of the tumors. I became increasingly depressed on behalf of the mice. Before I could convince Dave to terminate, we heard that two of the control mice had died on schedule and that the rest were in such poor condition they were expected to follow shortly.

Dave became even more optimistic about continuing. As he argued, "Perhaps the treatments are slowing down the cancer even if they can't prevent it. There's no record of a single mouse living past day 27. Get one to live beyond twenty-eight days and we'll have a world record. Experiments rarely turn out the way they're supposed to. That's why they're called 'experiments.'"

Great! So now we had lowered our sights from cancer prevention to a statistical study comparing longevity in two sets of pitifully dying mice. I asked one favor: "Since all the mice are going to die anyway, can I see the control mice?"

Dave arranged a visit through the biology chairman and the assistant. It was a somber sight. The four remaining mice were huddled together, eyes dull, skin shrunken, coats scruffy. Though their growths didn't have the blackened spots I had noticed on my mice, they were so enormous that all the mice were having trouble breathing. As I turned away, I wondered how I had found myself trapped in such a dismal cul-de-sac. Obviously, I didn't have the stomach for a career as an experimental biologist.

For a long time afterward, I couldn't get those control mice out of my mind. I kept visualizing them, cringing in misery, wishing I could help. By comparison, my own mice no longer looked so bad. Their coats were healthy and they remained frisky despite their tumors. Perhaps I could get one or two of them to day 28, when we would terminate the experiment.

By days 17 to 21, some of the tumors with their blackened spots had ulcerated. Though I assumed this to be the beginning of the end, the behavior of my mice had not changed. They were still cavorting as if nothing was wrong. This continued even after the ulcerations grew large, raw, and red, as if holes had been burned into the mice. Every day I wondered how many would be dead. When I found them huddled motionless, I would gently tap the cage, counting as one head after another looked up. Just asleep—this time.

By day 28 all five were still alive. I informed them aloud that they were making history. Privately, I wondered if the biologists would dismiss this as a fluke, or even suspect fraud.

I noticed another change in three of my mice. The inside of their ulcerations had turned from red to white. Though I assumed this was infection, I found no pus or other discharge. Was it my imagination, or were their tumors also shallower? During the next week the same whitening happened with the other two mice. More startling, I was now convinced the tumors were shrinking. As I watched day by day, they completely disappeared, and the mice's fur regrew. My patients now looked the same as when we had begun—little brown creatures of normal shape and size.

Dave and I were too stunned to jump to conclusions. Instead, he took the mice to the biologist for an expert opinion. We spent the evening together awaiting her report, pacing like expectant fathers, reprising the emotions we had experienced during the previous weeks— anxiety, disbelief, fear, foolishness, impatience, wonder, dread, frustration.

When the phone finally rang, I had to sit through a full repertoire of "yesses," "uh-huhs," and "oh I sees" while waiting for Dave to finish. After he hung up, he walked right past me, mumbling something I couldn't understand and looking ill.

I ran after him. "What's wrong?"

He ignored me while compulsively rubbing his hands and letting loose a string of expletives.

At last I got it out of him—"The mice are cancer free. They're cured!"

I ran around the apartment as aimlessly as a mouse on a wheel. I didn't know what else to do. Sure, I had witnessed many gratifying clinical healings, but curing mice in a laboratory was metaphorically like finding the smoking gun.

8. Too Good to Be True

"All truth passes through three stages: first, it is ridiculed; second, it is violently opposed; and third, it is accepted as self-evident."

—Arthur Schopenhauer, nineteenth-century German philosopher

After hearing the test findings, Dave and I didn't see each other for a several weeks. I think both of us needed to put some space between ourselves and those stunning results by letting our ordinary lives take over. No matter how much you might wish for something like this, when it actually happens it's just too much. The verdict on the cancer remissions put me into sensory overload. Even after the initial adrenaline rush subsided, I found myself uneasy talking about it. I needed a mental vacation.

I tried to keep busy by reading and puttering, including setting up a home aquarium for the cured mice, which I had grown quite fond of. At least I had saved them from their intended postexperiment fate—the maw of a laboratory snake. Now as I watched them spin the

wheel in their self-contained little world, with no apparent memory of recent trauma, my old ghosts returned to
haunt me. Since I had been "validated" as a healer, did
I have an obligation to publicly offer my services? The
more I thought about it, the more convinced I was that
scientific studies were the way to go. I felt confident
that Dave and I could unravel the mystery of healing for
everyone through systematic investigation.

In hindsight, my thinking was incredibly naive. I had
no concept of the difficulties to be faced. If I had, I might
have quit right then and there.

Despite my disinclination to spread the word, news of
our successful experiment reached Ben and his group. As a
face-saving spin, Ben now claimed that he had backed out
of the experiment to show that his techniques were so powerful even I could learn them. In a later version, he declared
that I had bumped him because I wanted the glory. Before
my "defection," some of Ben's patients had begun to ask for
me because Ben was becoming too theatrical, too embit-
tered. This only proved Ben's new contention: that I was
planning a coup to take over his group.

Because I considered Ben to be my friend and mentor,
I was aggrieved to learn that absence had only made our
relationship more hostile. I decided it was best for both of
us to keep our distance. Perhaps I still imagined a reunion
somewhere up the road. Given all we had shared, it was
hard to believe that this might be our final parting.

When Dave and I finally did review our mice experiment, we both knew that scientific rigor demanded we replicate our too-good-to-be-true results. This became even more pressing when we learned a confounding piece of new data: the four control mice had not died within twenty-four hours of our visit as the lab assistant had predicted. Instead, their tumors also developed blackened areas leading to ulceration, whitening, shrinking, then full remission!

As I struggled to make sense of this, I flashed back to the Dallas letter and Ben's other successful absent healings. When Ben was slated to do the lab treatments, he had insisted the control mice be kept in a different building. Did he instinctively understand they might be healed by proxy? Though I had not visited them longer than ten minutes, I had brooded over them afterward, picturing them in their misery and wanting to ease their suffering. Had I inadvertently done so?

Switching back to my discussion with Dave, I ever so casually initiated the hidden agenda I had brought to his office. "Sure, we need to replicate, but I think we should make enough procedural changes to get new information." Even more casually, I added, "To begin with, I don't think I should do the healing."

Dave was startled. "But where are we going to get another healer?"

"I already have someone in mind."

"Who?"

"You."

"You're joking!"

"I'll teach you. If I can learn, so can you."

Of course, he protested. "Maybe you had the ability all along. It just took Ben to trigger it. I couldn't possibly do it. I have no talent."

"It's worth a try. If it doesn't work, I can always do the next experiment. Think of the implications if this stuff can be taught."

Dave let that sink in. "Okay, but not me alone. We need backups. I'll pick another person and you can pick two. Maybe one of us will be able to do it."

I left Dave's office with my hidden agenda still hidden. I knew I should be included in the healings to see if I could repeat my own results, but I wasn't prepared to climb aboard that emotional rollercoaster just yet. I didn't want to be the healer endowed with unique powers. The Freak. The Mutation. Once again, I caught myself sympathizing with Ben's desire to clone himself in order to spread the weirdness around.

My success in passing the torch left me with a practical dilemma: where to find volunteers for the ridiculous task of remitting cancerous mice? Answer: Where does any professor look when wishing to prove or disprove a pet hypothesis? Why are so many academic studies skewed by the overrepresentation of a certain class of participant?

Of course: students.

I approached candidates selected for their intellectual curiosity, confessing up front that I wanted them for a healing experiment involving cancerous mice. I also explained that I had some hands-on techniques that I would teach them over the next six weeks, after which they would be expected to devote an hour a day during the month of the experiment.

Of my six potentials, one said he had seen a healer work and was eager to participate. Two others thought it was a great idea and wanted in. One was ambivalent. Two laughed in my face.

I chose the two who laughed because I wanted to eliminate faith as a factor. These two—a sociology major and a history major—not only didn't believe in hands-on healing, but later accused me of using this quasi experiment as a cover for some other undisclosed study. Though it took persuasion, I finally got them to agree.

Dave's choice of a healer came as a big surprise: the chair of the Queens biology department, Marvin Wasserman, also in his mid-forties, with solid credentials in his field as a widely published researcher. Though Wasserman had been indifferent to our first experiment, he was impressed by the reaction of the associate biologist who set it up. Apparently she had come into his office, deeply shaken by our results, literally begging him to tell her what we had done to achieve them. For a couple of decades, she had been conducting traditional studies on the same mice with the same injections, without being able to achieve anything like a remission.

I asked Wasserman if there was any chance our remissions could have been a fluke . . . that maybe the cancer hadn't taken hold.

"No," he assured me. "These mice are specially bred to have no resistance to the cancer. There are even specific strains of mice matched to specific cancers. The injections always take."

My four volunteers met in my apartment for our first training session. The students seemed impressed that two distinguished professors were participating, since I was apparently too young to carry the mantel of legitimate authority. They remained suspicious that the real study had nothing to do with healing mice.

I described the flow of energy that I had experienced while treating the cages. I then attempted to explain Ben's and my mental-imaging technique, beginning with the creation of a personal wish list, followed by its use in cycling. I also explained that the purpose of cycling was to distract the conscious mind from the healing work of the hands, allowing them to move naturally, instinctively, unconsciously.

After my belabored explanation, I introduced the group to the laying-on of hands. Standing behind each in turn, I placed my hands on his or her shoulders, then described the flow of energy as it coursed from my left hand through that person and then into my right hand.

Afterward I had them treat each other, hands on shoulders for about fifteen minutes to get the feel of that other person. Next they were to move their hands in search of hot spots to be treated.

Cathy the sociology major, Jackie the history major, and even my buddy Dave insisted there had to be more to the healing process than I was describing. When they complained of not feeling anything, I reminded them that my purpose was not to convert them into believers, but merely to induce them to follow instructions. Marv never asked a single question, though he was attentive, let me treat him, then fulfilled my request to treat the others.

As homework for the next week, I asked each participant to prepare a list of twenty wishes and then to practice cycling. They were also to spend at least four hours laying on hands with any willing subject—pets, partners, whom- or whatever.

Our next week's meeting was frankly discouraging. None of my volunteers had a list of twenty items: Cathy had fourteen, Jackie had seventeen, Dave had eight; Marv said he hadn't made a list because he didn't understand how.

Swallowing hard, I repeated my explanation, reminding them of their promise to follow my instructions to the letter. While their lists would always remain private, I now asked each to add an image summing up the successful completion of our experiment. When no one could think of any, or even seemed to understand why we should do this, I suggested we all envision the five of us in this apartment toasting each other with champagne.

Again we practiced the laying-on of hands. All claimed to have tried it at least once during the week. Cathy and Marv thought they had experienced some tingling in their hands; Dave and Jackie had felt nothing.

All our remaining sessions were equally uphill. Dave repeatedly stated that he knew he couldn't heal. Marv was unusually quiet. The students didn't bother to hide their conviction that they were wasting their time. They had no sense of mastery of the technique, and no way of measuring improvement.

When I announced that the mice had arrived, Cathy confessed she was terrified of rodents—a fact she didn't think necessary to divulge so long as she still thought I was gathering data for a study on student gullibility. She agreed to continue only if she could put a brick on the metal lid of her cage.

At the end of our last meeting, I gave the group a pep talk like a coach before a championship game, pushing myself hard to appear upbeat. The prospects for anything positive coming out of this seemed dismal. Even though I wouldn't be seeing a mouse during the whole experiment, hands-off was proving as nerve-wracking as hands-on.

The mice were being prepared by the same biologist who set up the first experiment. Each person was to receive two mice in a single cage, to be treated an hour a day except on Sundays. I asked everyone to keep a daily log of any changes in the mice or in themselves. Marv had arranged for the students to use the lab of a professor who was on sabbatical. He and Dave would look after their own cages. The control mice were somewhere on campus in a place known only to Marv and the biologist. We were to continue our weekly meetings. I also encouraged everyone to call me anytime, day or night, with questions.

Two days into the treatments I received a hysterical call from Jackie. When she had gone to the lab after classes, she had discovered that one of her mice was dead. I tried to calm her, explaining these things happen, even though I felt just as devastated. She explained that she wanted out of the experiment. Silly as it might sound, she had grown attached to the mice and found it too much to bear. I told her, quite honestly, that I still remembered the anguish I felt when I thought my mice were dying, and I apologized for putting her through this. Reverting to my role as researcher, I asked her to take the dead mouse to Marv's lab for analysis, then persuaded her to continue treating the other one.

I was not looking forward to our next weekly meeting. With one mouse already dead, what reason did I have to assume the others would survive?

Jackie and Cathy arrived first, as usual. Cathy was trying to comfort Jackie, who still wanted out of the experiment. They were like mourners at a wake. I remained respectfully silent.

When Dave and Marv crashed this somber scene, they were smiling. "We've got good news," reported Dave.

As Marv explained to Jackie, "Your mouse died of natural causes. It only had one lung. Physical defects aren't unusual with inbred laboratory animals. Since mice have high metabolisms, they have to be perfect to survive even under ordinary conditions. A mouse can't make it on one lung."

"You mean it didn't have cancer?" I inquired.

"I didn't say that. We found a tumor, but it was far too small to have caused death."

Jackie was visibly relieved. "But what about Frak? Does he have two lungs?"

The guys in the room, myself included, looked at her in puzzlement. "Who's Frak?"

"My other mouse. Frik was the one who died."

"You named them?"

Cathy responded indignantly. "Of course we named them! Mine are Genevieve and Suzanne."

With this drama having run its course, I asked the volunteers to report on their experiences while treating the mice. Marv and Dave said they hadn't felt anything in their hands. Neither had Jackie, though she noticed her mouse kept gravitating toward her left hand no matter how she placed the cage. Cathy had felt a tingling.

I asked each volunteer in turn to hold out his or her palms, facing downward, an inch above mine. Heat radiated from deep within each of their left hands—not just heightened skin temperature, but something qualitatively different. Once again, only Cathy sensed hers warming up.

After they left, I felt excited about the experiment for the first time.

By our next meeting, all the healers reported visible growths on their mice. Though Dave and Marv were expecting this, Cathy and Jackie were clearly concerned. I explained that tumor growth was normal, but deliberately omitted mentioning the black spots or ulceration, preferring to let them make their own observations. This time when I checked their hands, everyone's again emitted heat, though only Jackie and Marv reported sensations.

Before our next meeting, I received an anguished call from Cathy. She was sure Genevieve and Suzanne were dying. Some of the fur had fallen from their tumors, revealing ugly black marks. Again I assured her this was expected. She was angry that I hadn't warned her.

I was now receiving daily calls of alarm from Cathy and Jackie, reporting that their mice's tumors were growing larger and ulcerating. As well as their emotional attachment to their mice, these were high-achieving students who were not used to failure, which was why I had chosen them. Knowing what to expect, Dave and Marv took the same process in stride.

At last, the good news began to trickle and then flood in. The ulcerations were turning white, filling in, and shrinking. All seven mice remitted.

It was then Marv reported his showstopper: four of the six control mice had also remitted. After two mice had died, he had started visiting them on a regular basis— a breach of our agreed-upon protocol. They were, after all, in his lab.

While Marv and Dave had not written logs—you can assign only so much homework to senior professors!— Jackie and Cathy had done so. I was struck by how closely their experiences paralleled mine. I was also struck by their dominant feeling of pessimism, better described as "hope against hope." This, clearly, was not faith healing.

Here are entries from Cathy's log:

Day 1: At times I felt happy and others sad. My hands had pain but I was tense and felt it was related to the pain. I tried to cycle at points of frustration and points where I felt the experiment would not work. I have a terrible tension headache. The longest hour of my life.

Day 5: Quite nervous because I saw the beginning of tumors. After watching I think it might only be on Suzanne. Tried to cycle but had much difficulty. Kept thinking I don't want them to die. Tried to read my cycling list but got nervous and wanted to call Mr. Bengston for reassurance.

Day 6: I think both mice are now showing tumors. I feel scared.

Day 8: Genevieve is more active than Suzanne. Really enjoy watching them. They are becoming more a part of the family every day.

Day 10: The tumors are becoming more pronounced on Suzanne. It looks like she is carrying around a small ball. Genevieve's is round and sort of pointy. My feelings about recovery: positive.

Day 14: Still doing very little cycling. While I treated the mice I read my cycling list whenever I felt the experiment would not work. Genevieve and Suzanne both have large tumors. Suzanne's is like a small ball under the skin. I hope they don't get much worse because I don't want them to suffer. Even prayed a little for them.

Day 15: Saw an ugly black mark on Suzanne. Called Mr. Bengston. He said the mark is normal and is a good sign. I don't believe him. I'm afraid I'm not doing it right.

Day 17: My feeling as I came home today was that one of them would be dead. I know how Jackie feels now. My hand hurt during the treatment. Probably tension. As I treated I got the feeling they would get better. I really want them to live.

Day 20: Both of them have ugly sores on the tumors. I don't want them to suffer. Feel like calling Mr. Bengston all the time.

Day 23: Had the feeling Suzanne wasn't going to make it. Tried to cycle as I treated. Genevieve active; Suzanne awake but still. I want this to end. Splitting headache.

Day 25: Tonight I noticed both Suzanne and Genevieve gnawing at Suzanne's tumor. It left a hole I could put my finger into. It was a sick sight . . . didn't want to look. Poor treatment . . . the hole got me very upset.

Day 26: Tonight I had a feeling of doom. I think I feel this way because I haven't really been cycling. Hope to revise my list.

Day 29: Suzanne's tumor seems to be shrinking. Didn't feel very much of anything as far as sensations. Working on new list for cycling. A little fearful about being too sure. Please work.

Day 31: I've really lost any sensation in my hands. I feel extremely unconfident. In school I haven't done well. Feel like it's a lost cause but will keep trying.

Day 34: Genevieve's tumor seems smaller. Suzanne's tumor definitely smaller. Maybe this will work. Afraid to hope.

Day 36: Felt good today. Treatment felt sort of back and forth. Started getting nervous as to whether they would get better. Tumors seem white inside.

Day 40: Tumors still shrinking. Want to believe they are going to get well but I am getting very impatient. This way and that.

Day 42: No change in the girls. I am very doubtful at times. I think I'm afraid I will fail.

Day 45: Suzanne's tumor almost gone. Genevieve's still there. Trying to be optimistic . . . hope she's all right. I really want someone to tell me they're fine so I can be sure.

We celebrated the success of the experiment as I had suggested—toasting each other with champagne. Despite the students' joy over their victory and their relief at healing their mice, they were traumatized by the experience. It was just too much. They felt troubled over what to do with their newly discovered abilities and how to fit them into the rest of their lives.

Again, I could empathize.

9. Enigmas

"You see, wire telegraph is a kind of a very, very long cat. You pull his tail in New York and his head is meowing in Los Angeles. Do you understand this? And radio operates exactly the same way: you send signals here, they receive them there. The only difference is that there is no cat."

—ALBERT EINSTEIN

I WAS ENTHUSIASTIC ABOUT MIDWIFING a third experiment featuring new questions and new controls. So was Dave Krinsley. Marv Wasserman was not. He had no scientific framework in which to place our tests. His specialty was fruit flies. If we could design an experiment around those, he might consider it—but not mice.

I was determined to follow the data provided by the mice.

I approached Carol Hayes, chair of the biology department on the Brooklyn campus of St. Joseph's College, where I was also teaching. Known as a good and demanding instructor who ran her department with authority, Carol made it clear from the outset that my mice proposal was not the sort she was usually asked to consider. To this day I can vividly remember sitting in her office, explaining my experiments as she struggled to keep a straight face before erupting in laughter.

It wasn't until I mentioned Marv Wasserman that I detected some possibility she might agree. She respected Marv. Because he had participated, she might consider doing so. Nevertheless she remained extremely skeptical, even openly mocking. If my mice had remitted, then something must have been wrong with the protocols.

Carol presented two conditions: she herself would do the procedure, and she wanted to pick the volunteers. After some bargaining, we settled on her choosing three while I would choose two. Though I would have nothing whatsoever to do with the mice, once again I would train the volunteers and we would have weekly debriefings.

Cathy, the sociology student from my last experiment, wanted to participate again. Her natural skepticism had reasserted itself, to the point where she had begun to wonder if I had switched mice on her. I also chose a child-study major using the same criteria as last time. Jane was a high-achiever and a nonbeliever who had no experience with hands-on healing. I never discussed Carol's criteria with Carol, but upon meeting her three biology candidates, I could see her standards must have been different from mine. While they had no knowledge of hands-on healing as I had hoped, they seemed so perplexed, so lacking in motivation, that I suspected they found their conscription less than flattering.

The first dilemma we wished to address in this next experiment—our third—was the curious habit our control mice had of remitting. As before, we had six control mice on site in a location unknown to the healers. To prevent the mere proximity of a healer from effecting a cure, Dave suggested sending a second group of control mice off campus. Carol agreed, subsequently shipping four injected mice to a colleague in a city unknown either to Dave or myself.

The second dilemma we wished to address was whether or not each individual was responsible for curing the mice in his or her care, or whether all the mice were being cured by one or two talented individuals. To gain further insight, we gave each of our five volunteers one mouse to treat at home and one to treat in the lab. My assumption was that if any one of our volunteers could heal, then all the mice in cages that were sitting in a row on a bench in the lab should remit, whereas the ones they took home would depend on each individual's ability to heal. To prevent the domestic mice from contact with other volunteers, we set up a precise schedule for each person to collect his or her mouse. Carol was to look after the six on-site control mice. This was our most elaborate experiment yet, and when the results came in, they flummoxed me. The four off-site control mice had died well within twenty-seven days as expected. Three of the on-site control mice had died while three had remitted. This seemingly ambiguous result seemed explainable by the fact that once again the proto-cols had been broken. After three of the mice had died, the biology students had stumbled upon them in their lab and began dropping in on them.

All the mice tended at home had remitted, suggesting that all five volunteers were capable of healing. The puzzle was this: the three mice the biology students had treated in the lab had died. If they could remit their mice at home, and they could remit the on-site control mice merely through casual contact, why couldn't they remit their lab mice?

I remembered an experiment that Bernard Grad had conducted using first-year medical students who were highly skeptical of all forms of mind-body healing. When they treated surgically wounded mice using hands-on techniques, the mice's rate of healing was consistently slower than that of a control group, which received no laying on of hands. This was interpreted as a confirma-tion of the "nocebo" effect, in which a treatment fails because of the negative attitude of the doctor.[1]

Perhaps my skeptical biology students had felt the same embarrassment I had felt, huddled in my storeroom and being sure to lock the door so no one would walk in on me. I even remember smuggling my mice up the stairs that first day so as not to encounter anyone on the elevator. All this subterfuge, and I wasn't even operating on my home turf or inside my own professional specialty! As biology students, shanghaied into participating, they might have harbored complicated feelings of resentment. Then there was the boredom of sitting hour after hour with hands glued to a mouse cage.

By contrast, when the biology students encountered the control mice, for which they felt no responsibility, they had no reason to feel any tension or resentment. As for those they took home, perhaps they had even grown fond of them as pets.

This, of course, was after-the-fact speculation. The truth was, I couldn't make scientific sense of what had happened. Nor could anyone else to whom I related the data over the next few years, including the Great Grad. It would take a eureka moment, more than a decade away, for the results of this experiment to create a breakthrough theory.

Meanwhile, I was eager to do a fourth experiment and so was Carol, simply because she didn't believe our results. Two other students, who had participated in previous experiments, also signed up for the same reason—sheer disbelief—while one of the biology students, who had failed to remit his lab mouse, wanted to try again. In addition, I chose three other skeptical students, for a total of six.

Because of my suspicions about the impact of psychological factors, I decided to make this fourth experiment much mellower for the volunteers. It was summer; they had no classes and the lab would be predictably hot. I provided a sign-up sheet, leaving it up to them to decide how faithfully they would attend to their mice.

This laid-back approach was just an act. I was intensely engaged, and when I found my volunteers skipping about half their treatments, I became very upset. Though I maintained my charade, I was experiencing the power-lessness of parents watching their kids compete, feeling greater anxiety than the kids, who can at least exert control through action. Or not.

As for the mice: by now the pattern and rate of cure was so well established that it was reasonable to predict that any one that developed black spots would go on to ulceration and remission. Carol and I, therefore, decided that all the mice—cured and uncured, experimental and control—would be sacrificed on the thirty-eighth day for the purpose of autopsy. By then, those that were going to die would have done so; the rest would be at different stages of tumor growth, blackening, ulceration, and full remission.

Even though I hadn't treated these mice, watching them die was hard. I told the volunteers the experiment would be terminated on the thirty-eighth day without explaining why, then made a point of being present for the dissection. Afterward Carol sent tissue samples to a colleague at an histology lab for independent assessment.

Of the eleven treated mice, ten had remitted or were in the process of doing so. The single exception had not developed the blackened area and had died on day 30. Autopsy revealed a big, rock-hard cancerous tumor—clearly a failure of the treatment. Seven of the eight on-site control mice had remitted or were in the process of doing so—once again, they had been visited by the volunteers, this time under the relaxed protocols. The four off-site control mice had all died within the predicted twenty-seven days.

Histologic analysis (the microscopic study of thinly sliced tissue) found mammary adenocarcinoma cells at every stage of remission, proving beyond all doubt that we had been remitting cancer. Only those mice whose ulcerations had completely closed were cancer free. By now I knew that the mammary cancer we had been injecting was even more lethal than I realized. Any mouse that lived to day 27 was a Methuselah. Most in the biological literature had died by day 20.

By any fair-minded assessment, our four experiments had proven that 87.9 percent of our cancer-injected mice had far more likely been cured by hands-on healing than through natural remission. This result was achieved despite the fact that Carol, unbeknownst to me, had double dosed some of the mice going into the last experiment. Even more promising: the histology tests, showing cancer cells at all preliminary stages, were a recognizable sign that the key to cure was immunological response. Previously I had assumed we had been killing cancer cells. Now I strongly suspected we had been stimulating the mice's own immune systems to fight the disease.

This theory was greatly strengthened when I learned that Carol, once again unbeknownst to me, had reinjected a couple of the cured mice from the third experiment, only to discover that the cancer hadn't taken. The treated mice, it appeared, had developed an immunity!

I felt overwhelmed with questions, new and old. Since these last cures had occurred with much less treatment, what "dosage" was actually necessary? If not an hour a day, what about ten minutes? Once the process had begun, was it self-perpetuating?

What role did distance play in remission? In all four experiments, a total of 87.9 percent of the treated mice had remitted; 69.2 percent of the on-site control mice had remitted; 0 percent of the off-site mice had remitted. If distance was a factor in the failure to remit, how far was too far? Was it the only factor, or did some other condition as yet undefined exclude the off-site mice from treatment? Asked another way: What connected the on-site mice so that what affected one affected most of the others? If such a connection existed, what broke it, accounting for the 12.1 percent failure rate even among treated mice?

Alternatively: Was healing the result of some kind of group consciousness among the volunteers? Had they collectively cured the mice, or did one or two talented volunteers account for all the successes? Is healing a special innate ability, or can it be taught to almost anyone?

Most intriguing of all: Were the mice cured through immunological response? If so, could that immunity be passed on to others through a vaccine?

When I approached Carol, eager to design more mice experiments, I found she was unwilling to proceed. Though she declared our results the most amazing she had ever seen, like Marv Wasserman she didn't know what more to do with them. They didn't fit into her personal career goals or into the ongoing work of her department.

Though I was disappointed, I understood. What we were doing presented a threat to traditional biology. My day job as a sociologist was well enough defined that any leakage about my "hobby" could be dismissed as eccentricity. The same was true of Dave Krinsley, who continued to lend moral and financial support for the mice experiments. We were just playing in someone else's sandbox. Carol and Marv were taking a professional risk for what would sound to most of their colleagues like unscientific hocus-pocus. History had already shown that ours was a field in which no success would go unpunished. Who could blame anyone, without a passionate, personal commitment, for walking away?

Carol and I did enjoy one final collaboration before severing our professional relationship. Like me, she had theorized from the histology results that the mice's immune systems were somehow involved. This intrigued her enough to suggest a completely different, very inventive experiment. Not with mice. With carrots.

Since the college didn't have the equipment to do serious immunological studies, she designed an immunological test that would work by default. Apparently plants—including carrots—also get cancer, roughly defined as uncontrolled cell growth. Though this activity sucks nutrients from the host, it isn't lethal because plants, unlike animals, don't have organs to destroy.

For what I called our "salad series," Carol introduced cancer into slices of carrots in a petri dish. I then went through the same training process with volunteers, some of whom had participated in previous experiments, trying to get them to cure their carrots of cancer. Since carrots don't have an immune system, I was hoping the experiment would fail; however, I deliberately indoctrinated the volunteers into thinking this was something they could do because it had been done before. I also tried the same experiment myself, working very hard to make the cancer disappear.

We all failed, which was good news to me. We had demonstrated by default that the laying-on of hands had not cured cancer in an organism without an immune system. The carrot slices had developed elaborate root systems, as if trying to grow back into carrots. Something was being affected, but not the cancer.

After that small but tantalizing success, I decided to quit my cancer research. Few professionals were willing to believe our experimental results, although these were unambiguous. The idea that the laying-on of hands might cure cancer was too revolutionary, especially among doctors and scientists trained to believe it couldn't be true. To continue, I needed the support of those scientists, complete with lab facilities, mice, and the proper protocols. Without their help I would hit the wall.

I chose to remember that I was really a sociologist. Like Carol and Marv, I decided to focus on my day job, including professional research in my own field.

Another couple of decades would pass before I again picked up the experimental trail.

10. Time Out

"If the man doesn't believe as we do, we say he is a crank,
and that settles it. I mean, it does nowadays, because now
we can't burn him."

—Mark Twain

My son, Brian, was born on September 24, 1980. A race took place between my wife's giving birth and my defending my doctoral dissertation from Fordham University on an aspect of criminology. My wife and Brian won by one week. We were then living in Northport, Long Island, about forty miles east of New York City. Our daughter, Elizabeth, was born there three years later. I was teaching research methods, criminology, and the sociology of religion and science at St. Joseph's College in Brooklyn as well as at a satellite campus in Brentwood. This required a lot of commuting. In 1979, I volunteered to teach exclusively at St. Joseph's newest campus in Patchogue, about sixty miles east of New York City on the south shore of Long Island Sound. Eight years later we moved into the nearby village of Port Jefferson.

A historic shipbuilding seaport, Port Jefferson is a very privileged community, where a single power-plant pays 51 percent of the village's taxes. That leaves plenty of money for an enriched educational system and excellent health-care facilities. Extra perks include access to more than four miles of beach and free membership in a country club on a bluff overlooking the sound, with a PGA golf course and eight tennis courts. I proudly call myself a welfare recipi-ent because I couldn't afford my lifestyle anywhere else.

Most residents of Port Jefferson are hypersocial and hyperactive. I was on the school board for six years and the library board for ten. These activities, along with my aca-demic duties, which came to include chairing the human relations department, easily filled the space left by my retirement from healing research. I had a new set of pro-fessional priorities and a growing family. When I looked back at that other life, driven by obsession, I felt the relief of someone who has escaped from a passion for which the price proved too high. I was no longer a modern King Canute struggling against the tide. It felt wonderful just to be normal.

As a salute to my former double life, I introduced a new course to the college curriculum called Sociology of the Paranormal, which I still teach. Instead of the weird dabblings in the occult that my students had expected, it was a sneaky course on methods and statis-tics applied to paranormal research. When my students complained, "We thought this was supposed to be fun!" I perversely replied, "This is fun, and if you're dealing with offbeat hypotheses, you'd better get your methodological act straight."

While keeping a low profile as an energy healer, I continued to treat relatives and a few friends. I cured my brother of tinnitis, which is noise in the ears without an external source. I also cured him of extremely painful diverticulitis, which is caused by small pouches forming on the wall of the intestines.

My kids had one thing in common—both were unusually healthy. Beyond that, they had been different in every way right from birth. Brian was a monster in size, in the 98th percentile, who developed into a quiet, easygoing star athlete. Elizabeth, who was very small, in the 2nd percentile, started elementary school with the highest score on standardized tests in the history of our district.

When Elizabeth was about five, an incident occurred that indicated she might be "different" in the same way as Ben and myself. I had just parked the car for Brian's Little League game when Liz began to scream. She had caught her hand in the car doorjamb. As I took her crushed finger in my left hand, she stopped screaming. A few minutes later she begged, "Stop squeezing my finger!"

I showed her that I wasn't squeezing. "See, there's space between my fingers and yours. Your finger hurts because it's healing."

We stood there for about ten minutes. When I took my hand away, Liz moved her finger. Finding it normal, she announced, "Okay."

The whole experience was such a spooky replay of Ben healing my girlfriend's finger that it gave me goose bumps. I particularly remember feeling something unusual in the energy between us—a sensation of specialness that would later be reinforced.

This was also the period in which I treated Laurie, the sociology student with breast and lymphatic cancer whom I wrote about earlier. When anyone asked me about payment, I never knew how to respond. At first I would say, "Whatever you think," then I requested $45 a treatment "if you can afford it." Recently I cured a man of neck cancer in return for a homegrown zucchini! My healing work has never been about the money. I have always wanted to give this knowledge away. I would love to find that everybody can do what I do.

In another case during this same time-out period, I broke one of my ethical guidelines and lived to regret it.

Though Marie wasn't a good student, she was a lively, articulate young woman whom everyone liked. Because she was flunking, she decided to join the army to get GI credits to continue her education later, when she felt she'd be more mature. Before leaving campus, she dropped by my office in a highly disturbed state of mind. As she explained, "The army gave me a physical and they found I have this fucking brain cancer. They said I'm going to die." With great force of will she added, "I'm not going to die! I'm going to beat this thing."

Marie didn't know anything about my healing work, but I admired her spunk. After she left, I was arrogant enough to treat her about a dozen times at a distance without her consent. Because we were no longer in touch, I had no information about how she had fared.

From time to time over the next few years, I wondered about Marie. One day a colleague, who sometimes tracked down students to see how they were doing, gave me Marie's phone number. We met downtown for dinner. When I asked Marie about her health, she told me, "What happened was quite amazing. I had a spontaneous remission shortly after I saw you. The doctors couldn't find any cancer at all."

"That's terrific!"

"Yes, but they didn't believe the results so they gave me radiation anyway. Now I'm sterile, but at least that's better than being dead."

I felt stricken. Even if Marie had known about my treatment, she might have opted for the radiation, but she would at least have done so with knowledge. After this experience, I elevated asking for permission to heal from an ethical guideline into an ironclad rule.

One of my toughest cases was Georgina, a severely depressed nurse in her mid-forties who had been on medication for twenty years and was essentially nonfunctioning. She had no job. She had no interests. She had no friends or family besides her sister, Helen, one of my colleagues who was a clinical psychologist. When I met Georgina she didn't even talk, and of course Helen had already shopped her to every doctor and therapist she could think of.

I treated Georgina for an hour once a week for about ten weeks, with absolutely no effect. When she did start to come to life, I tried to get her to cycle, but she was incapable of thinking in terms of independent wants and needs. In fact, the more she improved, the more upset she became because then she realized that health brings responsibilities. Georgina had to be retrained just like someone who has emerged from a twenty-year coma. Six years later, Helen was able to report, "Georgina has become a real person!"

Another colleague introduced me, tragically, to the Pauline Effect. As a college administrator, Pauline had always been supportive of my mice experiments, even to the point of attempting to get foundation money for me. When I heard she had cancer, I went to her office, quietly shut the door, and explained that I wasn't just a mouse specialist. I had also cured dozens of people with cancer. I told her I'd be honored to treat her, but the choice had to be hers alone.

Though Pauline possessed an imposing personality, she stepped back with what I can only describe as a nervous giggle. It was clear she didn't know what to do with my suggestion. Rather than taking this path less traveled, she opted to go the traditional route, which soon led to her death.

The same thing occurred more recently with Julia, a professor from California. When we met, she had just published a double-blind study on the effectiveness of prayer in a conventional medical journal—a real breakthrough for her and for the field. We had discussed joint research possibilities, but when she didn't get back to me on schedule, I wrote it off as another case of initial excitement that had dissipated. Later I learned Julia had been diagnosed with brain cancer. She too had gone the traditional route, and she too had died. It was a very aggressive form of cancer, which I had successfully treated a number of times, leaving me to wonder: What, no phone call? No request for help? Even more mystifying, Julia's father had previously been cured of cancer by an energy healer, and Julia taught my work on hands-on healing in medical school as an official part of the curriculum!

These two cases showed me the difference between intellectual acceptance of energy healing and a willingness to defy the strong cultural bias against it when the chips are down.

One general truth I have learned through hands-on healing is how out of touch many people are with their bodies. Though I'm as guilty as the next person of taking my own good health for granted, I have a lot of physical control when

I want it. As a kid I was a competitive athlete, especially in and around water. I could also wiggle one ear at a time to the envy of my friends, flare a single nostril, cross my long toe over its neighbor, fold my fingers back to my wrist, and beat drums with considerable coordination.

In college I played tournament ping-pong, and that's the fastest ball game there is, with the ball whizzing at you 110 to 120 miles per hour. You can't play that game consciously because you can't see the ball—it's too fast—yet somehow, after years of practice, you can hit it.

Professional athletes in peak condition often speak with wonder about being in the zone, as if describing a grace period outside time and space in which they can accomplish the seemingly impossible. Occasionally when I'm playing tennis, the ball looks so huge as it sails across the net that I feel I can do anything I want with it. Healing is sometimes like that. When you're in the zone, in the flow, or whatever you want to call it, it's as if you're outside yourself watching yourself; however, just like a professional athlete, you have to do the work first to achieve that mysterious alchemy of concentration while letting go.

I'm sometimes asked how effective I am at healing myself. Until a few years ago, I didn't even know what a headache was. One day when I suddenly felt a strange pain in my head, I thought, *Oh, this is what that word means.* Then I made it go away.

I didn't seriously take up tennis until I moved to Port Jefferson. Then I soon got into trouble because I was trying to play on swimmer's legs. A butterfly competitor strengthens the up-and-down thigh muscles, whereas a tennis player pulls them in a different direction because of constantly moving from side to side. I was a fish trying to be a mammal, and the conflict was ripping my knees apart. When I consulted a couple of orthopedic surgeons, they advised scraping out my knees and giving me an operation—not a very tempting offer.

On a hunch I pulled aside Elizabeth, who was then about thirteen, and instructed her, "Fix my knees."

"How?"

In another echo of my experience with Ben, I replied, "Just put your hands on them."

"But what am I to do?"

"Quit asking questions. Just do what your hands tell you."

Liz started moving her hands around without any confidence at all. Suddenly she said, "Wait! I should put them here. Is this right?" That wasn't the place I had been complaining about, but when she homed in I could feel astonishing things coming out of her hands. It took about three treatments for me to be completely cured, and I haven't had any knee trouble since.

Throughout this whole process, Elizabeth claimed not to feel anything, but she's the most naturally gifted healer of anyone I have ever known, including Ben and myself.

As a little kid, she would come up behind me and take me by the shoulders with these disproportionately strong hands only inches long. I would feel the healing coming out of them and just go, "Wow!" We don't talk about this in our family. If Liz wants to follow the healing route, it has to be something she chooses on her own.

On another occasion, I was hanging out with a friend in Southampton, eating pistachios by the pound, when suddenly I doubled over in pain and my stomach started to expand. As I drove home, I became so bloated I had to take off my belt. That night I alternated between shivers and fever, but instead of going to a doctor, I kept thinking, how long can this last? Eventually I passed out from the excruciating pain. When I came to, I drove to the hospital and literally crawled into the emergency room. I was diagnosed with gallstones, for which the doctor recommended immediate surgery. I decided instead to make the gallstones go away. Back home, I enlisted Liz's help. Once again, the pain disappeared, and I have been symptom free ever since.

I should confess that my retirement from mice research during this layoff wasn't 100 percent. Helen, the clinical psychologist whose sister I treated for depression, tried in dozens of places to get grant money for me. If she had succeeded I most certainly would have continued, because it was banging my head against a wall of rejection rather than the research that had exhausted me.

I also became involved in one more mice experiment—the fifth— with Dave Krinsley serving as healer. Dave had been lured from Queens College in New York to Arizona State University, which was trying to make its geology department internationally famous. A biophysicist friend of his, also at ASU, had received a large grant from the National Science Foundation to study the electrical conductivity of tumors. That friend was growing a cancer lab with all sorts of mammals, from mice to chimpanzees. Since he and Dave had a number of research interests in common, he told Dave we could do one of our mice experiments using his facilities. After I flew to Arizona to help set it up, Dave did the treatment.

It was a disaster! Our one hundred mice remitted, but so did the mice in the friend's tumor study. So did the gerbils. So did the hamsters, all the way up the food chain. What we learned from this was that mass matters—the larger the animal, the longer it takes to remit. We also learned when to keep our healing hands to ourselves!

During this time-out period, Dave and I conducted a number of experiments in remote viewing, with obvious implications for distant healing, though I didn't make the connection at the time. The term "remote viewing" was introduced in the mid-1970s by Russell Targ and Harold Puthoff of the Stanford Research Institute. It refers to the process in which an agent (the sender) goes to a secretly selected place and views a target, which a percipient (or receiver) attempts to draw according to the images that appear in his own mind.

Sometime in the late 1970s I had read *Mind-Reach*, Targ's and Puthoff's bestseller,[1] detailing remote-viewing experiments in which the receivers' drawings seemed close to photographic representations of the targets viewed by the senders. Despite Targ and Puthoff's adherence to scientific protocols, I thought this stuff sounded too good to be true. So did Dave, proving how tough even those of us with "weird" in our curriculum vitae can be in assessing the claims of others.

Despite our skepticism, Dave and I decided to test the theory. Since he as usual claimed to have no psychic ability, I was to be the East Coast sender, while he would be the Phoenix receiver. We agreed to do the experiment on a specific summer day at 2 p.m. eastern daylight saving time, which would be 11 a.m. in Phoenix, since Arizona doesn't do daylight saving. So that Dave couldn't guess the target through familiarity with my habits, I asked someone he didn't know to pick one for me. She chose Crocheron Park, a place I had never been before, suggesting that I arrive fifteen minutes early, then wander around until two o'clock. Whatever I happened to be looking at would be the target.

I did as suggested. At zero hour I found myself staring at a gazebo. Because this predated the Internet, I was to draw the target and mail it to Dave the same day. Dave, who was supposed to be sitting in his office receiving, would follow the same protocol so that our drawings would crisscross in the mail. Since I can't draw a straight line even with a ruler, and Dave is just as artistically impaired, we seemed like a good match.

Using a yellow legal pad, I quickly and crudely sketched the gazebo, then took it to the post office.

Two days later Dave phoned, all excited. "Did you get my drawing?"

Since I hadn't yet opened my mail, I rifled through the pile on my desk until I found what looked like the right envelope and ripped it open. As I stared at the drawing of a gazebo on a sheet from a yellow legal pad, I experienced a disconnect. "Oh man, we've broken the protocol," I said. "I've got my own drawing back."

I picked up the envelope. It was addressed to me in Dave's handwriting. "Wait a minute!" I reexamined the drawing. It was Dave's all right, but so much like mine, line for line, including the coincidental use of a yellow legal pad, that I could have superimposed one on top of the other. By then I had also discovered Dave's second page. It read, "You got to the target early. You wandered around following a path that wound like this [another accurate drawing]. The sky looked like this [a third accurate drawing]." Typically, Dave signed off, "I don't think this worked. I didn't really get anything."

This test had an even more provocative postscript. According to the notation on Dave's drawing, he had confused the hour. Instead of sitting in his Phoenix office receiving at 11 a.m., which is 2 p.m. New York EDT, he was receiving in his office at 2 p.m., which is 5 p.m. New York EDT. I know what I was doing at five o'clock, and I wasn't in the park drenched in sunlight staring at the gazebo. Though I had stayed for a while because it was such a nice day, I'd left for the post office when clouds began rolling in. We can get very violent thunderstorms in the summer, and I was at home listening to music when this one struck. I disconnected the record player and all our other electrical gadgets as we're supposed to do. By five o'clock I couldn't even stand near the window because of the catastrophic rains and wind shaking the glass. That's when Dave was "seeing" the beautiful blue sky I had been looking at three hours earlier.

According to Targ and Puthoff, remote viewing is supposed to grow easier with practice. Not between Dave and me. We peaked on our first try, though one of our failures proved more insightful than if it had played out by the book. Once again I had a friend pick a target—an unmanned electrical plant, about twenty yards by twenty yards, fenced off from the road. On a rainy Saturday, I drove there at the designated time. I stood under my umbrella staring at it while listening to the electrical buzz, then painfully drew it and mailed it to David.

By then he and I had loosened the protocols so we could talk on the phone as long as we had both posted our envelopes. Uncharacteristically, he called me that evening full of confidence. "I know that I got it!" he exclaimed. "It's a motel."

"You're wrong," I told him. "Not even close."

Dave wouldn't back down. Finally our ranting grew so loud my wife came into the room to find out what the fuss was about.

I told her, "My target was that electrical plant past the waterfront restaurants, but Dave keeps insisting it's a motel. He's even arguing about it."

"But there's a motel right across the road," she said.

"No, there isn't." Now I was arguing with her. To prove my point to both of them, I got back in the car and drove to the electrical plant. Damned if there wasn't a motel right across the road! It had been behind me all the time I had been staring at the electrical plant. Being a task-oriented male with tunnel vision, I had done exactly what I was supposed to do without noticing anything else.

When Dave's drawing arrived, he had sketched the motel exactly as I had found it with the bushes, the walkway, the roof—everything. Since he couldn't have been reading my mind, it was as if he had actually seen the target in some creepy way with his own eyes.

After that we had some partial hits and a few complete misses—at least, that's how it appeared, though if I had been alone in the house when Dave saw the motel, I would still be insisting he was totally wrong then as well.

I mention these remote-viewing experiments with Dave because I know that, even for people who accept hands-on energy healing, distant healing requires yet another leap of faith. I understand that because it still astonishes me. That's why I held out against the idea of remote viewing, despite the Targ-Puthoff evidence. Without a personal test, the scientist in me was just as unwilling as any other garden-variety skeptic to make the connection between distant healing, with which I was familiar, and remote viewing, with which I was not. In hindsight, it's probably an example of my left brain being unwilling to acknowledge, without its own kind of proof, what my right brain already knows.

In remote viewing, as in distant healing, "something" is happening between two people across time and space that allows information or energy to be exchanged in mysterious and intelligent ways, which so far defy the analysis of conventional science.

11. More Moonlighting with Mice

"If I want to stop a research program I can always do it by getting a few experts to sit in on the subject, because they know right away that it was a fool thing to try in the first place."

—CHARLES KETTERING, American inventor

BY PERSUADING ME TO JOIN the Society for Scientific Exploration (SSE) in 1999, Dave Krinsley effectively ended my sabbatical from cancer research.

Founded in 1982 by fourteen scientists and scholars, the SSE is a multidisciplinary organization committed to the rigorous study of unusual and unexplained phenomena. To become a full member, you must have a doctorate or the equivalent; an appointment at a university, college, or other research institution; and a record of scholarly publication.

Today the SSE has eight hundred members in forty-five countries. Because they are dedicated scientists whose curiosity extends beyond their own disciplines, and not just New Age dabblers, I agreed to deliver a paper on my cancer research at their 1999 annual meeting in Albuquerque, New Mexico. Given the unpredictable, often hostile response to my work, I had no idea what to expect as I faced the auditorium of about 125 scientifically informed people. After my presentation, I waited nervously as everyone silently stared. Was this a good stare, or was I in danger up here?

The first question came from psychiatrist Richard Blasband, a former faculty member of the Yale Medical School, who is now in private practice. As a researcher, he had worked at the Jackson Laboratories, which had supplied my mice. "What are these ulcerations you're talking about?" he wanted to know. From his own observations, mammary cancer just did not remit.

His inquiry was eager, not hostile, as were those that followed, especially from the biologists. Instead of refusing to believe, they were willing to actually look at my data, and afterward I was stalked by the editor of the peer-reviewed *Journal of Scientific Exploration*. That resulted in a paper—"The Effect of the 'Laying On of Hands' on Transplanted Breast Cancer in Mice"—published in the *JSE* in 2000.[1] It seemed to touch a nerve. I received lengthy e-mails from all over the world—from bioresearchers, chemists, physicists, psychiatrists. I still do.

Now reinvigorated, I accepted an invitation to speak to the New York Area Skeptics Society, knowing its members were intent on banishing any findings that strayed outside a strict, materialistic framework. Sure enough, the audience faced me in a united front, arms folded, with a permanent *harrumph* on their faces. When I finished speaking, they kept repeating some version of "That's ridiculous!"

I agreed. "Yes, it is. Have you found any flaw in my methodology?"

"Well, it just can't be."

"My thoughts exactly, which is why I kept replicating my experiments."

Afterward a few brave individuals did hang around long enough to say things like, "That really got me thinking," which was encouraging news, and later I received several e-mails from members asking to be kept informed. Most, however, continued to ignore the classic definition of skepticism: someone who doubts everything, including his own skepticism.

When the same society invited me back, I knew many members would be waiting patiently with their mice questions, so I decided to give them a completely different talk, based on data from the National Opinion Research Center (NORC), at the University of Chicago.

NORC—which produces the best surveys of non-institutionalized adults in the United States—was then directed by Andrew Greeley, an excellent sociologist as well as a priest and successful writer of popular fiction. In one General Social Survey, he threw in some questions about mystical experience, telepathy, and other paranormal phenomena, worded as neutrally as possible. As he explained in a 1975 monograph,[2] he couldn't understand why J. B. Rhine's well-conducted ESP experiments at Duke University, which he had read in the seminary, had been so controversial. This forced him to conclude that science—like the Vatican—was a faith-based orthodoxy.

Through Greeley's NORC survey, he discovered that 40 percent of Americans had had at least one profound mystical experience, in which they found themselves in touch with something indescribable that took them beyond time and space. Often they declared such events as the single most important in their lives, producing significant changes.

What startled Greeley was how few in his sampling had confided these emotionally charged experiences to any other person. Wives didn't tell husbands. Patients didn't tell therapists. These were ordinary folk who lacked the language or the confidence or the permission to speak about their supernormal experiences.

Greeley followed up this survey with psychological tests, in which he discovered that the people who had reported these mystical and other paranormal experiences—especially the multiple offenders—were among the happiest, the healthiest, and the best-educated in the population.

All of that became the basis of my second talk to the New York skeptics. Essentially I was telling them from their own podium that they were less successful, less informed, and not as well-balanced as their weird brethren. More *harrumphing*.

That was fun, but far and away the most exciting response to my SSE paper was an invitation from Dr. Pramod Srivastava, head of the University of Connecticut's Center for Immunotherapy of Cancer and Infectious Diseases, to speak to his medical researchers. Wall-to-wall bodies filled the hall, with others lining the corridors. This was my most challenging audience yet, because I was an interloper in fields ruled by these conventionally minded immunologists and oncologists.

Dr. Srivastava's introduction was exceptionally generous. "What you are about to hear is extraordinary. Always remember that the mindset of a real scientist is to follow the data even if the ideas don't seem to fit."

As before, the room was disconcertingly silent throughout my presentation. Afterward members of the audience grilled me for two hours, searching for flaws in my methodology. This was followed by a sustained ovation, with the French researcher who had given me the toughest time chasing me down the hall as my most effusive convert. More importantly, Srivastava invited me to spend a sabbatical at the University of Connecticut continuing my mice research.

UConn's Medical Center is a huge, well-funded operation with an extensive animal facility and dozens and dozens of research labs. I was especially excited about access to the Center for Immunotherapy. Given my encouraging findings that energy healing might be linked to the immune system, my long-term goal was to use hands-on healing with conventional research to develop a cancer vaccine.

The biggest hurdle to my accepting Srivastava's invitation was arranging a sabbatical from St. Joseph's College, because professors are supposed to apply well in advance. Fortunately, the college's administration has always been unusually supportive of my unconventional moonlighting. This proved no exception. Thanks to official permission and the generous efforts of my colleagues, a way was created for me to begin work at UConn the following fall, in 2002.

I eagerly set about designing nineteen research studies: What is the lowest dosage (shortest amount of healing time) needed to produce a remission? Is healing self-perpetuating once it begins? How does radiation impede energy treatment? Can a blood transfusion from a cured mouse immunize another mouse against cancer? And the big one: can a vaccine be created from that blood to produce immunization in others?

The first clue that I might not be as happy at UConn as I had anticipated came during an August meeting with Dr. Stanley Murphy (not his real name), who was to oversee my experiments there. When I pressed him for a date to begin, he seemed unusually offhand. "Oh, just come sometime after Labor Day."

"What experiment should we do first?"

"We'll work that out when you get here . . . By the way,

did you get a copy of my proposal to the IACUC?" He was referring to the university's Institutional Animal Care and Use Committee, established to ensure the ethical treatment of research animals. "They've turned us down, but don't worry. It's just a technicality. I'll appeal. Come anyway."

Whatever uneasiness this might have caused me was offset by the lighter side of this visit. When I mentioned to Murphy that mice with cancer automatically gravitated toward my left hand, he dispatched a grad student to fetch a batch of cancer-injected mice. As they pressed their tumors against my left palm, other students crowded around, peering over each other's shoulders as if watching a street magician. One even spun the cage to test the "trick."

"Healthy mice wouldn't have anything to do with me," I assured them, warming to the attention.

As I was leaving, Murphy offered another veiled warning: "I've been really curious about the response of people around here to your experiments. They seem so closed. They just don't want to talk about them, particularly the MDs." While I was weighing that negative information against my ovation, he added, "I'm going to be quite busy while you're here, but I'll try to keep in touch."

How to respond to this unexpected announcement? I remained too hopeful, too naive, to start connecting the dots.

***

In his initial invitation, Pramod Srivistava had offered me his private car and driver for the daily two-hour commute from Port Jefferson to UConn. I opted instead to stay Monday to Friday in a small hotel, paid for by the university.

At that time in my life, I had gone through a complicated divorce, which ended up with the kids living with me. After a few years I met Joann, a wonderful woman who would eventually become my wife. Joann and her children moved in with us just as my kids were about to go to college. Though we were a relatively new couple, she encouraged me to pack up and head for UConn, Monday through Friday, so I could concentrate on my experiments.

The week after Labor Day, I checked into the Homewood Suites in Hartford, Connecticut, then drove to the UConn Medical Center, where I was scheduled to meet with Murphy at two o'clock. He wasn't in his office, and his executive assistant didn't know where to find him. I was left to wander the halls of this big, ugly Kafkaesque block of a building, asking people if they had seen Murphy.

Eventually, his executive assistant relayed this message: "Murphy said to see Sam."

"Who's Sam?"

"The grad student. He has everything set up."

Now I was wandering the same maze looking for Sam. It took three hours to find him. When I tried to discuss the parameters of my first experiment, he just mumbled,

"I'll go get your mice." He returned wheeling three cages of white mice on a cart. "These can be yours."

Can be? "What's their story?"

"They've been injected with methylcholanthrene to induce sarcomas." That's cancer of the connective tissue, which is less aggressive than mammary cancer, meaning these mice could live twice as long—from forty-five to fifty days.

"Where will I treat them?"

"I don't know." Sam's attitude telegraphed: you've got your mice, so what more do you expect of me?

This time I was roaming the halls like a homeless person pushing a shopping cart, looking for some place to work. En route I encountered the French researcher whom I had converted from hostility to fervor during my UConn presentation.

"I want you to know that was the most amazing talk I've ever heard," he enthused once again. "If your research pans out, it will be one of the more remarkable findings in biology."

This was such a bright spot in my day that I asked, "Do you want to do any experiments with me?"

He stared at me in alarm.

I lowered the stakes. "Would you like to talk over lunch?"

He literally backed away.

That's how it went on my first day and how it continued every day for a month. I would go into a lab with graduate students working on their projects, and I would beg to use a bench. Next day someone would ask me to move on. As the attitude of the French researcher had signaled, the institution was freezing me out. Whenever I asked Murphy's executive assistant when I could see him, she would suggest an appointment "maybe" a month or two up the road.

My professional environment at St. Joseph's had always been exceptionally congenial, which was why I was allowed a sabbatical here in the first place. While the response to my mice research in other labs had sometimes been disappointing, this open hostility was new. Perhaps the fanfare with which I had been introduced had backfired. In the past I had always slipped in through the back door to work quietly in one department among many others, all pursuing divergent goals. Here, if my research succeeded, it could be interpreted as challenging the premises on which most other researchers based their work.

Meanwhile, I continued to treat twenty mice divided between four cages. To discover the minimum dosage for a cure, I had reduced sessions from sixty to forty-five minutes, along with their frequency. One batch of mice was being treated five days a week; one three days a week; one only once a week.

I was also trying to replicate one of Bernard Grad's experiments in which his psychic healer successfully employed the laying-on of hands to charge secondary substances, such as cotton, wood shavings, and water, to speed up the healing of surgically wounded mice. My choice was water, which I held in a container for forty-five minutes before Sam fed it to five cancer-injected mice whose whereabouts were unknown to me.

When I was a few weeks into this schedule, Dave Krinsley came to visit, excited to see firsthand this great opportunity I was supposed to be having. Since I had known well in advance the dates of his visit, I had set up an appointment with Murphy. For a couple of hours we sat outside his office like kids waiting to see the principal, staring at signs that read: "Before you knock, turn around and walk away" and "If you know what's good for you, you'll leave quietly." When I had been here in August, I thought these signs were a joke. Not today. Murphy was a no-show.

On day 34 of the mice experiments, I asked Murphy's assistant to inform him that I was quitting because every day at UConn had been a new adventure in humiliation. Suddenly a second graduate student named Conrad was assigned to me. I was also granted an immediate appointment with Murphy.

By now the five control mice were dying as expected, while most of my experimental mice were in remission, including those only drinking the treated water. Even Sam had quietly evolved from pained resignation to cautious interest. In fact, he and Conrad paid me the most sincere compliment I would ever receive at UConn. When I encountered them one day in the hall wheeling another researcher's cancer-injected mice, they dashed into a lab and slammed the door. Apparently they were afraid I might ruin the experiment by curing their mice with a single look or gesture.

Sam, Conrad, and I were sitting in Murphy's office when he walked in.

"What's happening here?" he asked amiably.

"Nothing that approaches experimental conditions or consistency," I replied. "Which is why I'm quitting."

Murphy is not only very bright, he's also very charming. "I don't understand," he said with engaging interest. "Tell me."

"That's the problem. You don't understand."

"Then let's review the data."

He seemed genuinely curious about the fact that some of my treated mice were now ulcerating—the first stage of remission. "That's never happened before with sarcoma-injected mice at UConn," he replied. "All of this is so encouraging."

"Yes, but I'm still leaving on Friday. I'm willing to return if you can give me a real lab; otherwise this is it." I added what I thought to be a modest request: "I'd appreciate it if you'd finish this experiment to see if the mice go into full remission. I'd also appreciate some photographs along with blood samples for immunological work."

Within a couple of weeks I received a phone call from Murphy's assistant, promising me a suitable place to work.

It was only a partial victory, because my mice had been killed without being photographed or having hemoglobin samples collected. From these incomplete results, I still felt confident in concluding that the laying-on of hands cured sarcoma as well as breast cancer, and that the charged water had been effective. While cutting down on treatment hadn't seemed to matter, I still didn't know the lowest threshold for cure. Obviously there had to be one. If I stuck my hand in Long Island Sound, all the sick lobsters weren't going to get better. If I washed my hands under a tap in a Manhattan hotel, the city's sewage system wasn't going to purify. There had to be a dilution effect.

In my second UConn experiment, I reduced treatment to thirty minutes and set up a complicated schedule whereby I treated more mice at the same time to see if increased numbers would increase the effect, decrease the effect, or make no difference.

On the forty-third day after the mice's injection, Sam and Conrad came looking for me.

"I have bad news," Sam told me. "Our experiments are being shut down."

Sam took my keys and walked me from the building, as per his instructions, and that was the end of my career at UConn. None of my phone calls or e-mails to Murphy asking for an explanation were answered. I never figured out why I had been treated so shabbily, or for that matter why

I had been reinstated after giving UConn every opportunity to get rid of me. My only clue came from Sam on the long walk out. Apparently, Murphy had been challenged for trying to override the authority of the IACUC, the university's powerful animal-protection service, which had never approved my experiments.

Sam and Conrad agreed to freeze blood from my mice that were now in remission, but I was never able to get my hands on the samples no matter how many begging letters or e-mails I wrote to everyone I could think of.

There is an unexpected footnote to this story. Four months after I had been ousted from UConn, Pramod Srivastava surprised me with an invitation to dinner at his home to meet a fellow scientist who was promoting a new book. This allowed me to set up an appointment to speak with him about my rocky reception at UConn. Though he offered no apology, he did confirm that the IACUC had been angry over the approval given to my experiments. While I was glad to be assured I had done nothing wrong, I was left to wonder if the real problem might have been allowing my sort in the door.

This was not paranoia on my part. After J. B. Rhine had piled up evidence for ESP, he was driven from the academic community at Duke University. Bernard Grad was so severely ostracized at McGill University for his energy-healing experiments that he couldn't even bear to drive by the institution after his retirement. In his 1986 bestseller, *Love, Medicine and Miracles*,[3] surgeon Bernie Siegel reported posting in a Yale doctors' lounge a positive double-blind study on the benefits of prayer by a San Francisco cardiologist. In short order, one of his colleagues scrawled across it "BULLSHIT!"

Among the old guard at the Society for Scientific Exploration, there's a standard rule for anyone wishing to do anomalous research, meaning experiments that are atypical and hence deviant. The rule is: "Get tenure first!" Recently I gave that advice to a biologist with a newly minted doctorate who wanted to do energy-healing research. The next time we crossed paths, he thanked me. By then he'd had the chance to discover for himself the wisdom behind my warning.

Science can be as faith based as any other belief system, with its priests and its heretics. In the modern scientific world, discoveries are usually made one small step at a time, based on firmly established premises. It's this approach that has led to the world of wonders all of us have inherited. Upheavals affecting the premises are rare, and such upheavals are fought out on a rarefied level until some rough consensus is reached. Then the new scientific theory can be presented to the laity as more revealed truth: the big bang, relativity, quantum physics.

Energy healing doesn't dispute the value of Western medicine, with its sophisticated use of technology. It does imply that it may not tell the whole story. Charismatic healers whose reputations are based on anecdote can easily be dismissed by trained researchers as naive or fraudulent; those of us who invade the laboratory may be seen as an insult or a threat. In attempting to find a cancer vaccine based on energy healing, I'm not wishing to debunk Western medicine. I'm simply trying to find a way of making what I have experienced fit together with what more conventional researchers do, thus opening up new fields of discovery.

In the end, my experience at UConn reminded me of what Ben said after he had cured the leg injury of my college friend, Walter from Nigeria, much to Walter's embarrassment: "Walter thinks of himself as an intellectual. He's a convert to the pursuit of the rational. Now I'm his tribal past that's haunting him. If you understand Walter's problem with hands-on healing, you'll understand why the scientific and medical communities will never go for it either."

I'm still hoping that Ben was wrong about that word "never."

12. From the Casebook

*"The living body is the best pharmacy ever devised. It produces . . .
everything manufactured by the drug companies, but it makes them
much, much better. The dosage is always right and given on time; side
effects are minimal or nonexistent; and the directions for using the drug
are included in the drug itself, as part of its built-in intelligence."*

—DEEPAK CHOPRA, endocrinologist and author

A PREDICTABLE RESULT OF MY going semipublic was a sudden increase in the number of people who wanted me to treat them.

Probably my most bizarre case was Jerry from Connecticut. As an X-ray technician who contracted out his services, he had an inexhaustible supply of doctors he could consult, including a number of psychiatrists who routinely diagnosed him as unbalanced and prescribed medications. He had also been having bloodwork done almost every week and had undergone so many X-rays I'm surprised he didn't glow in the dark. I didn't ask to see his records, but I knew he had been working his way down the clinical ladder until he came to me. From his demeanor it was clear that psychologically he was hanging by a thread.

As soon as I put my hands on Jerry's shoulders, I had the weirdest feeling. "I don't know how to tell you this. I sense something in your head. The best description I can give is that of a vibrating egg. The pointy end is slanting at about thirty degrees toward your eyes."

Jerry started to cry. "That's it! Nobody ever believed me. Phone my doctor! You've got to phone my doctor."

I could imagine the conversation. "I don't think that's going to help your case with him."

"Then I'll have him call you!"

And he did. A clipped, clinical voice informed me, "I'm phoning about my patient Jerry . . ."

I immediately began the defense. "This call was not my recommendation. I can only report what I observed." Despite my disclaimers, my explanation sounded surreal even to my ears. "I sometimes get sensations when I work on people. Coincidentally or not, they confirm what Jerry experiences."

Naturally, the doctor assumed I was as unbalanced as Jerry, or perhaps in collusion with him.

I certainly didn't believe, without evidence, that Jerry had a physical egg in his head. Perhaps the image was so vivid to him that he was able to convey it to me. Perhaps his brain was trying to make sense of some kind of neural experience the rest of us routinely filter out. In any event, the egg was real enough to profoundly affect Jerry's life. He was desperate, so I treated him once a week for quite a few months until he was cured. By then he had latched onto me, which occasionally happens, and I had to forcefully discharge him. I was afraid he might come back with something else—scrambled eggs, a whole omelet—but that didn't happen.

Jerry's problems reminded me of a case of spirit possession, real or imagined, that Ben and I cured many years previous. Tom and Ellen, a New Jersey couple, were absolutely convinced that Donny, their poorly behaved adolescent son, was possessed by a demonic spirit. They had felt its presence. They had seen it. So had Donny. I'm not sure who got the idea first, but by the time they called Ben and me, the situation was very intense.

When Ben began describing the spirit as an angry-looking boy, it was like a preview of my experience with Jerry and the egg. All three started shouting, "That's it! That's it!"

Since Ben and I weren't faith based, he attempted to persuade the angry spirit to seek out another spirit as a better match for himself and to leave the kid alone. That seemed to work. The parents were happy. The kid was happy. There didn't seem to be any downside—unless, of course, the spirit actually was demonic, and he and his new pal ganged up on someone else.

I lump these cases together because of their nonphysical elements. In our culture, we are programmed to seek out ministers and priests for spiritual help, therapists and psychiatrists for psychological help, and medical doctors for physical help, reinforcing the illusion that these are separate categories. Most practitioners soon discover that these fields overlap, giving them a choice between strict adherence to the rules of their discipline, or a certain flexibility in serving the real needs of their clients.

After a seminar in which I jokingly confessed that I had never been able to cure a wart, a dermatologist described to me how he had cured a patient who was covered with them. He instructed the patient: Take an apple. Place it like this. Cut it like this. Do this four times a day. To make sure the patient precisely performed the elaborate ritual, they practiced together in his office.

As the doctor hoped, and the patient expected, the warts soon began to disappear. The doctor had responded to the real needs of the patient, based on his own life experience and what he understood to be the patient's belief system. He had also taken a personal risk. If he had tried this routine on the next patient, he might have faced a malpractice suit.

While I consider flexibility to be a virtue, I also know my limitations—not necessarily those of the energy, but of me as a person and a healer. Sometimes when I touch people, they have flashbacks to events or emotions they have repressed. While I have no problem with their expressing these feelings, I leave the interpretation to others.

My most dramatic reaction to hands-on treatment came from a woman in her fifties who I can only describe as a tumor factory. As fast as they were surgically removed, others would grow in their place—all benign. Since Greta and I played tennis together, I could tell that she was sometimes in pain. By then, she'd had five or six operations, which hadn't solved her problem and had resulted in a mass of scar tissue.

Greta was a very private person with a diamond-sharp mind and complex eyes that looked out from a thundercloud that perpetually hung over her head. She had an extremely dark and traumatic past, having to do with the politics of another country, of which I was unaware when I offered to treat her. As I reached out to touch her in the sanctuary of her own home, she began shrieking, "Keep your filthy hands off me!" I was startled, to say the least. Her world and mine were obviously not the same.

After we both got over our shock, Greta mustered enough trust to allow me to treat her about a half-dozen times. I banished her latest crop of tumors, and as far as I know she never developed any more. Were Greta's tumors the result of her traumatic past, or were they caused by exposure to some toxic substance? Was my treatment physical or emotional? My best guess is that it might have been both.

I am sometimes asked if curing people of one ailment only leads to their replacing it with another. Perhaps. But if that's their need, they're canny enough not to return to me with the replacement symptom. Some problems, like alcohol or drug addiction, have obvious psychological as well as physical elements. With those, I concentrate on helping the person overcome his or her cravings, while insisting they work hard at cycling. If I'm treating you for a lump, you may get away with being passive, but curing addiction requires you to change who you are, and that needs constant reinforcement.

I'm still frustrated by people who quit treatments that are producing positive results. A colleague asked me to help a relative who had Lou Gehrig's disease, a progressive, wasting disorder that attacks muscles and nerves. After I treated Bert a few times over a couple of days, he was able to use a knife and fork to feed himself. He was astonished. My friend was astonished. But Bert didn't return for his next treatment. Eventually I received an e-mail saying he might be able to fit me in some time. That didn't happen.

For the record, as well as treating people and mice, I have also successfully treated a rabbit. One woman drove five hours from Philadelphia with her sick bunny, which I cured of whatever ailed it. Though I wouldn't expect a rabbit to return my calls, I never cease to be amazed when people I have successfully treated fail to respond to my follow-up inquiries, possibly because they've convinced themselves it was really the carrot juice that healed them. One friend, whose breast cancer I had cured, didn't want me to treat her husband, hospitalized for chest pains suffered while jogging. As she snapped, "Then both of us would owe you our lives!"

Far from expecting enduring gratitude, I file my healing experiences in a different neural cabinet from my ordinary memories, so I'm more inclined to forget a case unless something triggers my memory.

I'm always frustrated when unnecessary delay changes a treatable problem to one with an uncertain prognosis. This is especially true with injuries, because the situation is so dynamic. Whereas you didn't get Alzheimer's last Tuesday, that might have been the fateful day you fell from a ladder and broke your neck. Wednesday will be quite different from Monday. Time is of the essence because everything is still fluid.

I remember Ben and I treating a woman who had recently been blinded by trauma to her eyes. Monica could tell the difference between day and night, but she couldn't distinguish movement or shapes. Doctors had told her that the chances of her sight returning were not good. Within the first half hour of our first treatment, Monica pointed to her father and blurted out, "Person!" He was so moved he broke down sobbing.

Ben and I treated Monica once more that first day, and several times the following day. After that she could distinguish shapes and colors, allowing her to walk across the room without bumping into things. Eventually she regained functional vision.

I believe much of our rapid success was due to the freshness of Monica's wounds. We saw her within a week of her injury, before her brain and body had identified her as blind. Energetically, her memory and attitude was that of a fully functioning person with a temporary problem that just needed to be fixed.

Contrast Monica's case with that of Gordon, who had a ski injury that supposedly left him permanently paralyzed. A mutual friend, who sometimes does energy healing, thought Gordon could be helped, but only if treated immediately because the window of opportunity was a sliding one. My gut instinct confirmed that diagnosis.

Since distance was a factor, Gordon kept putting off his visit to me while exploring medical options closer at hand. Essentially, these well-intentioned procedures helped Gordon—once an athlete—to cope as a cripple: here's how to use your arms to lift yourself into your wheelchair; here's how to rearrange your house. By the time I did get to see him, more than a year had elapsed, during which Gordon had become his injury. He was a handicapped person rather than a well person trying to solve a problem, and I knew that a critical part of any treatment would have to be uncrippling Gordon's mind. This meant his envisioning himself standing up, walking around, even skiing, with cycling as a paramount part of the treatment. Unfortunately, Gordon was no longer up for that kind of challenge.

Kyle's case was yet another in which delay became a formidable enemy. He had been diagnosed with an aggressive form of metastatic bone cancer that I had cured a number of times; however, before we could set up an appointment, he booked himself into an experimental clinic in California. After that he went to Mexico for some drugs, then on to Santa Fe for a chemical cocktail of this or that. By the time he got around to me, he had grown so many cancers that his doctors couldn't count them all. He had also undergone chemotherapy. I treated him a couple of times but could do nothing for him.

My belief that I can't cure anyone who has had radiation or chemotherapy may be a self-limiting one. Perhaps as a healer, I have crippled my own mind through negative thinking. Whatever the reason, this illusion or reality lies at the root of some of my biggest disappointments.

Unlike Monica, who lost her sight through trauma, eight-year-old Jenny was going blind from a tumor on her optic nerve. She had received chemotherapy, and even though I treated her once a week for a number of months, I just couldn't get the energy moving. Since her parents were willing to do whatever it took, they flew her to Europe, then to Mexico, for experimental treatments. Last I heard, her sight was deteriorating.

Lucien's case was more baffling, at least at the outset. An interpreter phoned me from France on Lucien's behalf. Then the two of them flew to New York, where I treated Lucien over several days for what should have been a routine case of liver cancer. Even though something didn't feel right, and Lucien didn't seem to be benefiting, he invited me to Paris for more treatments. That's when I discovered how completely and perhaps dangerously I had been deceived. Not only had Lucien undergone chemotherapy, but he actually had a chemo pump implanted in his chest! Now, that's not subtle. My treatments might even have been undermining the effects of the chemo, giving Lucien the worst of both worlds.

A pleasant sidebar to my trip to Paris was an opportunity to visit Jacques Benveniste, an immunologist internationally respected for his research on allergies and asthma. Respected, that is, until some of his findings caused him to veer into alternative medicine.

While Benveniste was head of France's government-sponsored Institut National de la Santé et de la Recherche Médicale (INSERM), he accidentally discovered what became known in scientific circles as the "high-dilution effect." This means that water might retain a "memory" of a substance (antibodies, chemicals) that it once contained, even after being so diluted that not a single molecule of the original substance remained. He demonstrated this through an allergy test, which worked even when all the molecules of the allergen had been eliminated. As he summed up, "A person can enter a room two days after a cat has left it and still suffer an allergic response."

By extension, Benveniste's discovery supported the homeopathic belief that illness can be treated with solutions so dilute they appear to be pure water. This finding, replicated in a number of laboratories, caused an uproar in scientific circles.

Undeterred, Benveniste refocused all his INSERM research on proving that water can, indeed, carry biological information. As he indicated, the stakes were high: "This [the INSERM] is the only group that is researching at a basic level problems that affect 15 percent of the population. At the same time, one billion francs are spent on pharmaceuticals for allergy each year."

When more laboratories attempted to replicate Benveniste's findings, the results were mixed. The INSERM sacked him as a figure of scorn.

When I met with Jacques in Paris, he was working in a lab not much bigger than a trailer and scrambling for funding. At his request, I held a test tube of water for a few minutes, then gave it to a technician who scurried off with it. I was later informed that I had increased the amount of information the water could hold by about 50 percent—a finding mystifying to me, and so surprising to Jacques that he reported it to a 2000 SSE meeting in Amsterdam, where we met once again.

I was saddened when Jacques unexpectedly died in 2004, at age sixty-nine. In mourning his passing, *Le Monde* stated that the world of biology had lost "one of its most brilliant, original, and impassioned researchers." I hope this will be seen as the first step in rehabilitating the reputation of a courageous man whose final years proved, as Andrew Greeley previously observed, that science is a faith-based system with gatekeepers ever ready to persecute its heretics.

Bennett Mayrick in the mid-1970s

Bill Bengston

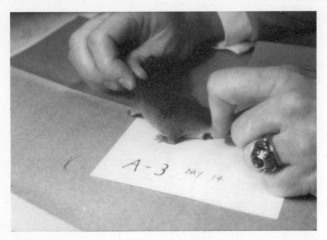

Typical mouse with mammary adenocarcinoma, 14 days
subsequent to injection

Same mouse as above, 28 days subsequent to injection and showing
the beginning of tumor ulceration

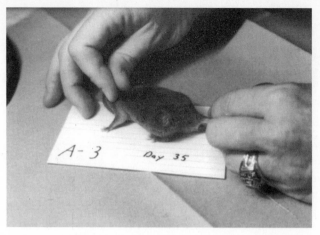

Same mouse 35 days subsequent to injection and showing full ulceration

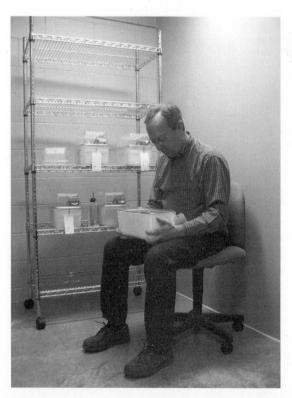

Bill applying
a hands-on healing
session to lab mice

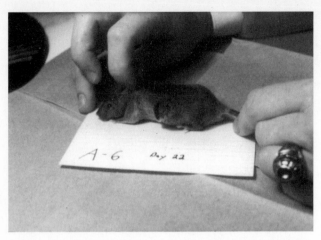

Example of very rapid-healing mouse, 22 days subsequent to injection

Same mouse as above, 6 days later, completely healed

13. Eureka!

"The most erroneous stories are those we think we know best—and therefore never scrutinize or question."

—STEPHEN JAY GOULD, American biologist

AS IT TURNED OUT, BEING FIRED from UConn benefited my mice research in a way I could never have predicted. Since I was still on sabbatical, I had plenty of time to brood. Though my seven experiments at four institutions had produced plenty of challenging clues, the big picture still eluded me. I was especially mystified as to why 100 percent of the control mice that were sent off-site had died as expected, while so many of my on-site control mice had remitted.

Ironically, the answer to that question, when it finally hit me, required me to think like a sociologist. I had chosen sociology over psychology as a career because I was fascinated by the underlying social forces that direct human behavior. To see these forces in action, one need only look at how individuals behave during riots, or the effect of peer pressure on patterns of consumption. While I was puzzling over my cancer experiments in terms of individual mice, the answer as to why so many of my controls had remitted eluded me. When I thought in terms of social forces, the answer became obvious.

My eureka moment arrived just in time for Christmas 2002. I literally bolted out of bed and began manically running around the house, compulsively talking to anyone I could find. Though neither Joann nor my kids could make sense of what I was saying, when I listened to myself, I could.

In the experimental design favored by scientists for the last two hundred years, it's assumed that when you divide test subjects into two comparable groups, those groups are distinct and independent. Therefore, if you give a drug or treatment to one and not the other, then the difference in the response of the two groups determines the effectiveness of the drug or treatment.

Judged by that classic yardstick, my experiments were only partially successful, since 69.2 percent of my on-site control mice had remitted, along with 87.9 percent of my treated mice, for a difference of only 18.7 percent. However, in previous tests all over the world, 100 percent of mammary-cancer-injected mice had died within fourteen to twenty-eight days. Clearly, something new and significant had happened during my experiments. Could the yardstick itself be flawed?

EXPERIMENT #	# OF MICE	# OF REMISSIONS	% REMISSIONS
1. Experimental mice	5	5	100
Control mice on site	6	4	66.7
2. Experimental mice	7	7	100
Control mice on site	6	4	66.7
3. Experimental mice	10	7	70
Control mice on site	6	3	50
Control mice off site	4	0	0
4. Experimental mice	11	10	90.9
Control mice on site	8	7	87.5
Control mice off site	4	0	0
5. Experimental mice	15	15	100
Control mice on site	15	15	100
Overall experiment	48	44	91.7
Overall control on site	41	33	80.5
Control off site	8	0	0

This was my eureka insight: spatial separation doesn't always mean independence. Though the treated and control mice were kept in different locations, something unseen must have continued to connect them so that whatever happened to the treated mice also happened to most of the control mice.

That solution had been staring me in the face for more than a decade, but thanks to my habit of compartmentalizing my two lives, I had missed it. Curiously, all the other researchers to whom I had posed the problem also missed it. While following protocol usually produces the most reliable data, sometimes you have to change, metaphorically, from freight train to jet plane to see the overall picture.

I began to review all of my experiments for which I had complete data in the light of my new theory, which I called "resonant bonding."

Experiment 1: Five of five of the experimental mice were cured. After I visited the control mice, the four out of six that were still alive subsequently remitted.

Experiment 2: Seven of seven of the experimental mice were cured. After one of our healers started visiting the control mice, the four out of six that were still alive remitted.

What connected the control mice with the treated mice, allowing them to heal? Was it the healers' empathy for the mice under their care, which was extended to the control mice by a physical visit, creating a single, bonded group?

Similarly, did resonant bonding also connect all the healers into a single, shared consciousness, combining both empathy and intention? If so, the treatment of any mouse by any healer would have been a treatment for all the bonded mice. This would include the control mice, following a healer's visit, which allowed them to remit despite their more advanced stage of disease.

That would also mean my attempts to determine which individuals could heal, along with appropriate dosages, were invalid. Once the healers had bonded, the healing work of any one could not be separated from the healing work of any other.

Alternatively, did resonant bonding occur among the mice themselves because of their shared experience of being inbred and raised together before being separated into groups? Did this allow at least some of the control mice to benefit at a distance from the hands-on treatment given to their genetic brothers and sisters?

Perhaps this is not a case of either/or, but both/and. Perhaps resonant bonding among the healers, among the mice, and between the healers and their mice, all merged to create a dynamic field of energy and intent.

Experiment 3 was more complicated: All five healers remitted the mice they took home. When three of the healers discovered and then began visiting the control mice, three had already died, while three remained alive. Those latter three also remitted. So far these results could be explained by resonant bonding, as already described.

All four off-site control mice died. This was not unexpected. If bonds can be created, then presumably they can be broken, accounting for this 100 percent fatality. Perhaps travel to a different locale broke their common bond of experience with the mice whose environment they once shared, as well as moving them outside the consciousness and caring of the healers.

The complication with this experiment arises from what happened to the five mice treated in the biology lab. While the sociology and child-study students remitted their two mice as expected, the three biology students failed to remit their three lab mice; therefore, of the ten treated mice, only seven were cured. What factors could account for this unanticipated failure?

In his McGill University experiments, Bernard Grad found that if psychic Oskar Estebany wasn't feeling relaxed, he couldn't heal. Since Bennett Mayrick's ability seemed unaffected by moods, I had argued with Grad against the influence of psychological factors. However, after my layoff from UConn, I had crunched some numbers comparing my first UConn experiment, when I felt angry and uncomfortable, with the second experiment, when I was reasonably happy. What I discovered was that my second batch of mice had fared far better in terms of tumor size and speed of remission.

Perhaps psychological factors also played a significant role in the work of the biology students. All three remitted the mice they treated in their own homes, where they presumably felt at ease; however, their discomfort while sitting in the lab in their white coats with their hands on their mice cages was reflected in their logs, in which they reported embarrassment and fear of peer ridicule. Perhaps this negativity broke their bond of empathy with their lab mice. Perhaps it also broke their bond with the non-biology-student healers, isolating their mice from the other mice successfully under treatment. Perhaps all three biology students even formed a bond of negativity with each other, further isolating their mice. This would confirm Grad's earlier findings that medical students, with professional reasons to dislike hands-on healing, actually retarded the healing of surgically wounded mice as compared to control groups of untreated mice.

Experiment 4: When protocols were relaxed, ten of eleven experimental mice were cured along with seven of eight on-site control mice, while all the off-site control mice died. Resonant bonding can account for all these results, except for the death of one treated mouse. I still have no explanation as to why one of our healers was unable to remit this mouse, especially since its companion in the cage went through the now-normal process of remission to full cure.

In the summer of 2003, I presented my first paper on resonant bonding to an SSE meeting in Paris. Midway through my talk, a group from a lab in Freiburg, Germany, began shouting, "You've solved the placebo problem!"

"That's terrific," I replied, "but I never knew there was a problem. What is it?"

Until then, placebos weren't on my radar screen because I considered them merely a phenomenon of human suggestibility. Now, at the urging of the Freiburg gang, I examined them more closely.

In a classic study published in 1955,[1] Dr. Henry Beecher stated that in fifteen trials with different diseases, 35 percent of 1,085 patients were satisfactorily relieved when treated with substances they thought were medically prescribed for their ailments. For example, patients suffering severe pain from wounds and angina experienced relief when injected with saltwater, which they thought was morphine. This has become known as the placebo effect—Latin for "I will please," referring to a patient's desire to please the doctor as an authority figure by getting well.

In a 1978 review of similar studies, psychiatrist Jerome David Frank of Johns Hopkins University School of Medicine concluded that at least 50 percent of the effect of any drug that influences patients' subjective state is due to the physician's expectations as transmitted to the patient—that is, at least 50 percent is a placebo effect. Harvard-educated doctor and biologist Andrew Weil was even more decisive in his 1983 book *Health and Healing*, in which he stated that the history of medicine is actually the history of the placebo response.[2]

Until fairly recently, medical researchers regarded all things placebo with feelings of mystification, dismissal, and outright annoyance. If 35 percent of people in a control group who are given a dummy pill are going to react as if they have taken the real thing, then the results of all drug trials using humans are going to be seriously skewed. However, I discovered that placebos are a lot trickier and more interesting than that. As detailed in "Resonance, Placebo Effects, and Type II Errors"[3]—an article I coauthored for the *Journal of Alternative and Complementary Medicine*—when drug trials are repeated, the placebo effect actually increases, so it's fairly common for dummy pills to mimic up to 80 percent of the results of the drug being tested. Even more supportive of resonance: this effect is proportional, so if you secretly increase the dose of the drug, some of the control patients will react as if the dosage of their dummy pills was also increased. So pervasive are these implications for drug testing that U.S. pharmaceutical researchers no longer attempt to demonstrate that a new treatment is superior to the effect created in the control group. The new standard is to prove that the tested drug or treatment is no less effective for the same condition than any existing treatment or drug already on the market!

By that standard, my hands-on healing treatments, with cures of 87.9 percent, when measured against a predictable 100 percent fatality within twenty-eight days, were an astounding success. Especially when you add the possibility of lifelong immunity, as suggested when my cured mice resisted the repeated cancer injections used to reinfect them. While I wouldn't want to underrate mouse consciousness, I don't think anyone could argue the placebo effect: my mice did not get better to please me.

14. Talking to Machines

"The Universe begins to look more like a great thought than a great machine."

—SIR JAMES JEANS, British astronomer

WHEN I WALKED INTO THE 2005 meeting of the International Society for the Study of Subtle Energies and Energy Medicine (ISSSEEM) in Colorado Springs, a couple of hundred people were sitting, eyes closed, chanting OM.

The ISSSEEM is a nonprofit interdisciplinary organization dedicated to exploring all forms of energy healing. Unlike the SSE, it has no stringent qualifications for joining, resulting in a broad-based membership ranging from highly qualified medical people to hands-on healers with no formal training. Since my paper on resonant bonding was more scientific than inspirational, I wondered if I had made a mistake in presenting here; however, the audience proved receptive, and through my new association with the ISSSEEM I have met several people who I hope will be lifelong friends.

Bonnie from Idaho is an oncologist who gave up her medical practice a dozen years ago to become an energy healer, because she thought she could do more good that way. Les, an Arizona internist, was about to give up his practice for the same reason. While he was taking standard case histories, he began hearing voices in his head offering additional information and even making diagnoses. When he asked his patients if the things he heard made sense, they said they did. To be true to himself, he decided to become a full-time hands-on healer. He regarded attendance at ISSSEEM meetings as an opportunity to learn healing techniques. After I explained cycling, along with how I move my hands, I offered my usual caveat about not knowing what parts of my process were critical and what parts were just a tool.

"What does it matter," Les asked, "so long as your patients are getting better? That's all that counts."

I gazed at him across the gulf separating the clinician from the researcher—the same one I had experienced with Ben. As I had been rediscovering at the ISSSEEM, the world of energy healers is divided between the clinicians who treat on blind faith and are perpetually reinventing the wheel, and researchers isolated in their laboratories who blindly follow the data without regard to its application or the practical discoveries of the clinicians. That bothered me then. It still does.

Thanks to my ISSSEEM talk, Margaret Moga, a doctor of anatomy, invited me to test resonant bonding at her lab on the Terre Haute campus of Indiana University School of Medicine.

We began our first experiment—my eighth—in 2005. Thirty mice were injected with mammary cancer—fifteen as controls and fifteen to be treated. Resonant bonding predicted that the control mice would respond in the same way as the treated mice. That's what happened. We had thirty remissions.

As a creative sidebar to this experiment, Margaret employed a geomagnetometer, which can measure fluctuations in the geometric micropulsations that are a constant part of the earth's magnetic field. When I tried to influence the probe directly by passing my hands around it or by touching it, nothing happened. When Margaret put the probe in the room where I was treating my mice, the micropulsations suddenly changed from randomness to coherence, creating a wave lasting a couple of seconds. The fact that I was not able to affect the probe directly but only through an organism, suggested once again that my treatments were being triggered by the biological needs of those organisms. These results have been published by Margaret and me in the *Journal of Alternative and Complementary Medicine*.[1]

We also experimented with distant healing. While my first three treatments were conducted hands-on in Indiana, I did the rest from New York and from Sedona, Arizona. To our surprise, the geomagnetic waves were at least as pronounced when I was in Sedona. Again, I have no explanation for this beyond citing psychological factors. In Sedona I liked to sit in a small church, treating a picture of my mice while gazing out onto an incredible landscape of red rock that changed with the sun. By prearrangement with Margaret, I would work from, say, 11 a.m. until noon, making note of any moments when I felt a special, qualitative change in my connection to the mice, as if all barriers between us were dissolving. Afterward I would phone her with the times—11:17, 11:44, and so on—and she would check the geomagnetic readings. In this way we found that the wave fluctuations corresponded to my subjective experience of resonant bonding.

I still consider it awesome to be able to connect with creatures hundreds of miles away. In fact, every time I cure a mouse I'm amazed all over again. With humans I'm one person working inside a field of possibilities, but when treating a cancer-injected mouse, we're both naked. I'm all they've got.

In our second Terre Haute experiment,[2] we confirmed the results of the first one, again using distant healing along with the probes. When it became apparent that all the tumors were progressing toward a cure, Margaret sacrificed some of the mice for anatomical examination. She then surgically implanted tumor fragments from those donors into eight mice that had already been cancer injected for a third experiment.

Now, a fatal mammary-cancer dose is about sixty thousand to one hundred thousand cells, but we had infected those eight mice with two hundred thousand cells, and then reinjected them. We really tried to kill them! Amazingly, only three of the eight developed tumors, when it should have been 100 percent. This suggests that the other five mice acquired some immunity along with the implanted tumor tissue from the treated mice. This is the closest I have come to my dream of creating a preventative vaccine.

Through the years, I have experimented with other measuring devices in hopes of illuminating what happens when I give treatments. Despite the boredom, the discomfort, the time, and even the travel involved, curiosity gets the better of me. I suppose I'm like anyone else seeking a diagnosis for a medical condition: if something about you appears abnormal, you want to know more about it.

Before my falling out with Ben, we briefly experimented with Kirlian photography. Invented by Semyon Kirlian in Russia in 1939, it uses a high-voltage, low-amperage electrical device to allegedly make visible the aura of an object that is in direct contact with a photographic plate. Auras, which appear as a pulsating glow, are supposed to reflect an organism's state of well-being. According to Kirlian, in one experiment a healthy leaf was shown to radiate dynamic flares, a dying leaf only dim ones, and a dead leaf none at all.

Although skeptics dismiss these effects as due to ionization, ultraviolet rays, aberrant electrical effects, and so forth, the concept of an energy field radiating from the human body is basic to Eastern medicine. Many people claim to be able to see auras without the use of devices, especially around the human head and fingertips, where they are supposed to be strongest. In cultures all over the world, drawings and paintings depict saints, angels, magicians, and shamans with radiating halos.

Before experimenting with Ben and me, the owner of the Kirlian device had placed his two fingers on a Polaroid film holder, then turned on the machine for two seconds. The resulting film, developed in sixty seconds, showed a faint bluish glow extending about an eighth of an inch from his fingers. After several other people went through the same process, this aura appeared to be typical for people in ordinary good health. When those with known physical problems were tested, the aura diminished both in length and intensity, roughly corresponding to what Ben and I already knew of their general health.

Ben's aura was not normal. Neither was mine. The glow from our fingers extended at least a quarter of an inch and was much brighter than the others.

I suggested that Ben treat one of his regular patients so we could compare before-and-after pictures. Choosing a woman with arthritis whose aura was the weakest of everyone measured, Ben treated her for fifteen minutes.

The resulting picture showed a dramatic improvement in her aura—even the owner of the Kirlian device said he had never before seen such a drastic change.

According to the literature, Ben's aura should have diminished as a result of giving away some of his energy to the patient, rather like water seeking its level. Instead, the aura surrounding Ben's fingertips had grown to almost half an inch and was white with intensity.

As a check, I treated one of Ben's patients for fifteen minutes. The change in both the patient and me was comparable to the previous experiment. Though this result was different from what we were told to expect, it corresponded to Ben's and my subjective feeling that hands-on healing invigorates rather than drains us. More significantly, it also suggested that we were accessing some external source of energy.

In the interest of science, I have also spent thirteen hours inside fMRIs (functional magnetic resonance imaging)— once for four hours at a stretch. If you have ever been in one, you know that it's a tight fit, with your head strapped down and perhaps with instructions appearing on a screen over-head. I'm not claustrophobic, but I am sensitive to sound. It's very loud in there, with lots of clacking and snapping, despite earplugs and noise-masking headphones.

fMRIs measure changes in blood flow and oxygenation as an indicator of brain activity. This is done by compar-ing on/off contrast states. For example, a subject might be instructed to think of a mountain scene and then stop, or to imagine reading an interesting book and then stop.

The first of my fMRI tests was conducted by Randy Benson, a neurologist, and Song Lai, a physicist, both then on the faculty at UConn. Usually shifts in brain activity are measured at around 2 to 3 percent, but when I was cycling in off/on mode, mine increased at least 25 percent in the visual part of my brain.

In one set of tests, I was lying inside the tube with my left hand sticking out. A technician would put an envelope into my hand, leave it for a few seconds, then take it away. Some envelopes were empty. Others contained strands of hair and small Polaroids of animals with cancer—dogs, cats, horses—supplied by a veterinarian. Though I wasn't trying to do anything in particular, once again my brain reacted in a dramatically different way when I was holding an envelope with the animal pictures.

From these tests, I theorized that I was unconsciously responding to a need while holding the photos of the cancerous animals. Since I knew beforehand that some envelopes would have pictures, you could say I had an intention to heal, but without any awareness of when to turn on that function. That happened automatically and involuntarily. This also confirmed my subjective experience of what happens during hands-on healing.

Another set of tests involved two volunteers—Leona, a woman I had cured of breast cancer; and Jerry, whom I had treated for the anomalous egg in his head. This was an inside/outside test as well as an on/off one. That meant sometimes I was in the tube while the volunteer was in another room, and sometimes the volunteer was in the tube while I was in another room. The idea was for me to alternate sending energy and not sending energy to the target person at two-minute intervals. Though the brains of both target people registered a change, Leona couldn't consciously make the connection, while Jerry, whom I knew to be unusually sensitive, always could. In fact, I was told that his brain patterns changed even as I was receiving instructions to turn on.

After looking at one set of test results, Randy Benson was so startled that he declared I must be an alien!

More recently, I have undergone tests with EEGs conducted in a Phoenix lab by Jay Gunkelman, an internationally recognized EEG (electroencephalograph) researcher. These were initiated and financed by Luke Hendricks from Minnesota, who e-mailed me because of his fascination with my work. The advantage of EEGs over fMRIs is that they measure electrical brain activity directly on a time scale of a millisecond rather than through blood flow.

For these experiments, I was hooked up with nineteen recording electrodes fitted to my skull, along with an ECG (electrocardiograph) to record my heart rate. A volunteer in another room would be hooked up with the same kind of apparatus. On the signal, "Go ahead," I would try to link up with the other person as if I were healing. Though it's a very artificial and distracting setting, almost immediately our hearts went into synch, something very easy to see since it was a gross observation. By contrast, brain samplings from the electrodes were taken every 500th of a second, resulting in a huge database requiring countless hours to analyze. Though it's more than a year later, I'm still receiving feedback.

One obvious effect was that my brain, somewhere in the back of my head, would go into sudden spikes carrying roughly a 7.81 hertz signal, meaning 7.81 pulses per second. I say "roughly" because sometimes the spike would be slightly off that figure. It was a clear and dramatic effect that occurred at intervals in the EEG tracing. Seconds later our volunteer in the other room would show the same spike in the same area of the brain.

After studying the 7.81 hertz spike, Luke announced, "I've seen this number before!" It turned out to be Schumann's resonance—a long electromagnetic wave, discovered by physicist Winfried Otto Schumann, that continuously circles our planet between its surface and the ionosphere. According to current theory, it consists of power generated by the lightning strikes that bombard the earth at a relatively constant rate.

From the evidence, it seemed that my brain was going into a resonance with Schumann's resonance, triggering the brain of my target person to do the same. Could this mean that my power source for healing was lightning?

Of course all this is highly speculative. We still can't prove that the spikes in my brain actually correspond with healing. Perhaps we're finding answers to questions we haven't thought to ask. Even if Schumann's resonance does prove to be the carrier wave for healing, how does consciousness latch onto it?

Both with framing these experiments and analyzing findings, a basic problem is that we aren't sure what we're looking for, and we don't have an extensive body of research for comparing results. Another problem is that everyone running these projects is a volunteer with a heavy professional workload, so results are slow in coming back to me. Nevertheless, initial findings in all of my EEG and fMRI experiments indicate some measurable interaction between myself and a test subject, with exciting implications. Luke, Jay, and I have recently published a paper on the EEG studies.[3]

15. "Why Haven't You Won a Nobel Prize?"

"You can recognize a pioneer by the arrows in his back."

—BEVERLY RUBIK, American medical researcher

I HAVE PAID ONLY CASUAL attention to other energy healers because most of their supporting evidence—as presented in books and seminars—is anecdotal, whereas my own obsession is with the underlying fundamentals of healing.

Many of these healers trace their lineage back to a single revered teacher. Reiki (Japanese for "life-force") was founded by Mikao Usui, who reportedly received his healing powers in 1922 after three weeks of fasting and meditation on Japan's Mount Kurama. Reiki healers, possibly numbering in the millions worldwide, channel universal energy, which is said to be infinite and intelligent. They channel this energy through their palms, which are placed on or near their clients to stimulate the client's own self-healing. Some Reiki masters say they can not only heal at a distance, but also backward and forward in time.

Therapeutic Touch (TT) is a Western-based healing system that has been taught to an estimated seventy thousand professional caregivers and is offered to patients in some North American hospitals. It evolved from experiments that Dolores Krieger, a professor of nursing at New York University, did with psychic Oskar Estebany, demonstrating that hands-on healing significantly increased hemoglobin in the blood of sick people, suggesting an immunological response.[1] As with Reiki, TT practitioners hold or move their hands a few inches from their patients, with the intent of activating their immune systems.

In the West, the most popular hands-on healing tradition is founded in the miracles of Jesus Christ, as written in the New Testament in John 14:12. After restoring sight and curing the lame, Jesus told his followers: "He that believeth in me, the works that I do shall he do also; and greater works than these shall he do."[2]

Among early Christian cults, healing was an ordinary part of preaching, often utilizing oil and water. European kings such as England's Edward the Confessor, who claimed to rule by divine right, exercised the royal touch to heal their subjects. Even Napoleon was said to have tried his own skills, to little avail.

Today, faith healing remains a popular part of the Christian Evangelical movement. It's also endorsed, with caution, by the Roman Catholic Church, which expects miracles from those traveling the path to sainthood. I have sometimes thought how convenient it would be for me to reclassify myself as a faith healer, especially when I'm asked in a doubting voice, "If you can do what you say you can, why haven't you won a Nobel Prize?"

The practice of hands-on healing as a medical rather than a religious or a magical rite goes back at least as far as the ancient Greeks. Hippocrates (circa 460 BCE) was known as the father of Western medicine because of his reliance on keen observation and the principle of cause and effect. He summed up his extensive healing experience this way: "It has often appeared, while I have been soothing my patients, as if there were some strange property in my hands to pull and draw away from the afflicted parts aches and diverse impurities."

In the sixteenth century, Dr. Theophrastus Bombastus von Hohenheim—known historically as Paracelsus—spoke of a magnetic, healing, solar force that swept in waves throughout the universe. "Munia," as he called it, radiated around the human body in a luminous shield and could be transmitted at a distance. Despite the many healings attributed to him, Paracelsus was derided by his peers and negatively immortalized in the epithet "bombastic," based on his birth name Bombastus.

Inspired by Paracelsus, Dr. Franz Anton Mesmer (1734–1815) was also credited with many startling cures, such as ridding a Munich scientist of paralysis, and a professor of blindness, simply by passing his hands over them. When his disciples discovered hypnotism through experimenting with his techniques, Mesmer's cures were dismissed as the power of suggestion. In the spirit of scientific Enlightenment, Mesmer's name came into derogatory usage through the word "mesmerize," with its connotation of undue influence.

After European medicine moved into the laboratory, a universal energy, often with magnetic properties, was rediscovered many times.

In 1791, Italian anatomy professor Luigi Galvani, an early experimenter in electricity, wrote of a life-force similar to electricity and magnetism, which seemed to radiate from the sun. It had an affinity for metal, water, and wood. It permeated everything, pulsated through the human body by means of the breath, and streamed from the fingertips.

In the nineteenth century, German scientist and industrialist Karl von Reichenbach risked his reputation as the discoverer of creosote and several other chemicals when he declared evidence for a new universal energy, which he called "od" after the Viking thunder god Odin. Od was in free circulation throughout the universe, and it permeated everything. It radiated in a luminous glow from the human body and was vital to health. It was concentrated in iron, sulfur, magnets, and crystals, and conducted by metal, silk, and water. Though confirmed by researchers in Britain, France, and Calcutta, od was eventually dismissed by orthodox science as a blemish on von Reichenbach's otherwise outstanding reputation.

In 1903, French physicist René Blondlot claimed to have discovered a vital force, both biological and universal, which he called "N-rays." This finding was also confirmed experimentally by other French researchers, who noted its many similarities to od. Like his forerunners, Blondlot was ridiculed by his peers.

In 1936, Otto Rahn, a bacteriologist at Cornell University, noted a biochemical radiation from living cells that played a significant role in growth, cell division, and wound healing. As he stated, "It may be surprising that radiations have not been recognized and proven conclusively before this. The reason may be sought in their very low intensity. The best detector is still the living organism."[3]

Around the same time, biologist Harold Burr of Yale demonstrated that all living systems—from trees, to mice, to men—are molded and controlled by invisible electrodynamic force fields that can be measured and mapped with standard voltmeters. He called them "fields of life," or "L-fields," and believed their voltage could be used to diagnose physical and mental conditions before symptoms developed. Burr validated this theory by comparing the L-fields of mice injected with cancer to control groups of healthy mice.

Burr's colleague, Dr. L. J. Ravitz, extended these finding to demonstrate that emotion was energy in motion. He described this energy as electrical and found a connection between low-energy states and diseases such as cancer, asthma, arthritis, and ulcers.

In the seventies, Fritz-Albert Popp, a German physicist, discovered that all living organisms constantly send out tiny currents of light, which he called "biophoton emissions." These were stable in their intensity unless the organism was sick. Cancer patients, for example, emitted fewer photons, as if their batteries were going dead. He also found that organisms used these light emissions as a form of communication.

After Konstantin Korotkov, a Russian physicist, developed sophisticated equipment for measuring Popp's bioenergy fields, Russian doctors began using his tests to diagnose illnesses such as cancer. When Korotkov measured the coronas of healers while they transmited energy, he discovered remarkable changes in the intensity of their emissions, consistent with what Ben and I discovered while working with a crudely constructed Kirlian device.

Just like religion, science has its martyrs. The most conspicuous of these in the field of energy healing was Wilhelm Reich, born in 1897 in Galicia, now the Ukraine.

Though trained as a Freudian psychoanalyst, Reich discovered through his clinical practice that neuroses were caused by emotional blocks that create muscular rigidity. In his view, cure could be achieved through body manipulations designed to remove those blocks by releasing streams of energy, rather than through years of couch talk.

After Reich was expelled by Freud from the International Psychoanalytical Society because of his heretical views, he was driven out of practice in Vienna, Berlin, Norway, Sweden, and Denmark. On relocating to New York in 1939, he began working as a self-taught microbiologist. Within living cells, he believed he observed the same streaming energy he had discovered in the bodies of his patients. During pleasure, cells expand; under stress, they contract. When comparing the blood cells of cancer patients with those of healthy donors, he found constrictions that he judged to be the result of long-term stress. Deprived of emotional stimulation, the cells had run down like batteries, leaving the whole organism vulnerable to disease.

Based on these observations, Reich developed a blood test for diagnosing cancer before the appearance of tumors, anticipating the Pap smear by more than a dozen years. While other microbiologists were still obsessed with finding a virus or some other toxin as the cause of cancer, Reich had hit upon immunological breakdown.

Reich then embarked upon the most controversial phase of his unorthodox career. As the result of both his microscopic and clinical findings, he claimed to have isolated an energy in free circulation that he called "orgone." Massless and weightless, orgone radiated from the sun and entered our bodies through the breath. Since Reich's experiments with mice showed that orgone was reflected by metal and absorbed by organic substances like wool and wood, he constructed a metal-lined wood box that he called an "orgone accumulator."

After successfully treating a number of so-called "hopeless" cancer patients with his orgone therapy, Reich founded the Orgone Institute Research Laboratories, which offered the rental of his orgone boxes at minimal cost. His medical critics, once merely scornful, were now outraged. With the encouragement of the American Psychiatric Association, the U.S. Food and Drug Administration began an investigation of Reich for cancer quackery. When Reich—with an arrogance fed by a developing paranoia—failed to defend himself in court with appropriate diligence, his books and papers were burned under federal supervision, and he was given a two-year sentence. He died in prison in 1957 at age sixty, a broken man.

Today, Reich's innovative approach to cancer, emphasizing immunological breakdown, is a medically respectable one. His massage techniques and theories of energy healing have inspired thousands of practitioners, many of whom have never heard his name. Yet in mainstream history, he's still dismissed as a crackpot. When I mention his name to therapists, some actually recoil.

One exception to this is my Society for Scientific Exploration friend, psychiatrist Richard Blasband, who unabashedly calls himself a Reichian. Over the decades, Dick has researched a number of Reich's theories, including an offbeat one of special interest to me because of my association with Ben. According to Reich, orgone energy can be manipulated to force clouds to form or to disperse, thereby affecting the weather. For this he invented a cloudbuster made of collapsible metal tubes. In demonstrations during the fifties, Reich managed to convince skeptical journalists on more than one occasion that he had ended the drought around Rangeley, Maine, where he was then living.

Blasband constructed a cloudbuster in an attempt to replicate Reich's results. After a few positive tests, he took his Yale mentor to a demonstration on Long Island Sound.

"Pick a cloud," he instructed, just as Ben had once told me.

After Dick performed a series of successful cloud busts, his mentor told him, "Blasband, don't ever do that again. Don't ever talk to me about this again, and don't ever tell anyone else about this!"

Remembering my own dismay as I watched Ben dissolve clouds, I knew exactly how the professor felt. I also knew how Dick felt, since my own successful experiments so often crashed against this same wall of unrelenting disbelief.

After the crucifixion of Wilhelm Reich, it took a courageous researcher to dare to follow the same path. Dr. Bernard Grad of McGill University was such a man. And just as Grad openly took his inspiration from Reich, so I took mine from Grad.

When I encountered Grad's research in an undergrad course in my senior year at university, I was struck by the rigor, precision, and simplicity with which he approached complex, anomalous problems, producing results that were irrefutable. So many people talk anecdotally or in the abstract about energy healing, but Grad was a real scientist, designing experiments with clear findings that could be reproduced. He was the single most important influence on my research, and whenever I felt backed into a corner, his pioneering spirit eased my sense of isolation. He became a mythic figure: the Great Grad.

We didn't have any personal contact until 1999 when Dr. Edward Mann, a Canadian sociologist whom I had met at an SSE meeting, gave me Grad's phone number. After I dialed it with some trepidation, a gravelly voice said, "This is Grad."

I replied, "This is Bengston," thus launching a series of stimulating conversations.

When I sent Grad a draft of my paper "The Effect of the 'Laying On of Hands' on Transplanted Breast Cancer in Mice," he had both a strong intellectual and visceral response. Though healing cancer-injected mice in a cage had seemed exotic to me, it was the standard model that he, as an oncology researcher, had used with a number of healers without achieving positive results.

When he read about my success, he began grilling me by phone. I would get a call at one in the morning: "This is Grad. Are you sure you used the code H2712 mammary cancer?"

"Very sure."

Click.

Twenty minutes later: "This is Grad. Did you ever use male mice?"

"Yes."

"But you can't use male mice. You can't keep them in a cage together."

"Sorry, Bernie, but nobody told me."

Another call: "They couldn't have been male mice. They'd kill each other."

"We've done it with male and female mice. When they're sick, they huddle together. When they're well, they mostly ignore each other."

Fifteen minutes later: "What was the composition of the cages?"

"Um . . . I don't know. They were mice cages."

"Were they metal?"

"Well, the tops were. The sides were clear plastic."

"You can't heal through plastic!"

"Sorry, but I didn't know that either."

Fifth call, no exaggeration: "Are you sure they were plastic? I've never been able to get effects through plastic."

"Bernie, they were plastic. I don't know what else to tell you."

In 2000, Grad and I met at the New York brownstone of the American Society of Psychical Research (ASPR), where he was a board member and where I had once taken Ben to be tested. Then in his early eighties, Bernie was a small man with a ready smile and a twinkle in his eye. He's also one of the humblest people I have ever met. The two of us went into the ASPR's library, shut the door, then began pacing manically around this big library table, exchanging information and arguing. Our connection was immediate, exhilarating, and amazing.

One of the things I argued against then, but have since conceded to Bernie, is that psychological conditions can affect the healer. A more practical lesson is that healing energy can be transferred to secondary substances such as cotton and water. This is a tradition that goes back hundreds of years, as demonstrated by the Christian concept of holy water.

A very recent example is God in a Bottle, given to me by a woman, Enid, who I helped treat for cancer of the big toe, diagnosed by doctors as requiring an amputation. Suzanne, one of the people I have been training to heal, brought this patient to me because she lacked the confidence to take full responsibility for such a serious case. Enid had also been treated by the well-known Brazilian healer, John of God, who had been giving seminars in the New York area. He had charged the bottle of water that she gave to me, which now sits in my refrigerator. Since

Enid was still raving about him, I couldn't understand why she didn't just use the water instead of bringing it to me. In any event, the amputation was avoided, though it's difficult to say whom or what to credit for her healing.

As I have already reported, in one of my UConn experiments I personally used only treated water to take one group of cancer-injected mice into remission. I also confess that I have recently encountered a demand for Bill in a Bottle.

Last January, Yury Kronn, a traditionally trained Russian physicist, invited me into his Oregon lab to experiment with an apparatus he claims infuses energy/information from any one system into another. I was to sit in the midst of his banks of electronic equipment holding a bottle of water, while he allegedly transferred some high-energy recording of me into the water. Though Yury is very secretive about this process, the wires he uses are so thick I can only imagine that the lights across Oregon dim when he turns on his equipment. Anyway, the resulting Bill in a Bottle is now being distributed to volunteers, with a suggested dosage of ten droplets of Bill to ten ounces of ordinary water. As always, I await the results.

In my own clinical work, I am far more attracted to hand-charged cotton as a potential carrier of healing energy, especially when distance makes one-on-one treatment impractical. In a fairly recent case, the effectiveness of the charged cotton was demonstrated by default.

Ruby, who was in her forties, had been diagnosed with ductal carcinoma, a form of breast cancer. Though I had successfully treated that condition many times, I thought Ruby's case might be more challenging than usual because she had massive doses of radiation for cancer while still a child. Her doctors had predicted she would grow up with deformities, but instead she became a world-champion weight lifter. We're not talking heavy-weight here, since Ruby is only about 4 foot 9—perhaps one effect of the radiation.

Because Ruby lived six hundred miles away, I treated her hands-on for two days either in her home or mine, then gave her charged cotton so she could treat herself between visits. About a year after she was medically diagnosed as cured, I was at her home when she asked if I would charge more cotton for her just to be on the safe side. As soon as my fingers touched the piece she handed to me, I felt a palpable lump in my armpit, accompanied by pain. When I put down the cotton, the pain went away. I asked Ruby if she had a lump in her armpit, but she said no. When the same thing happened a second time, I pressed her for more information. This time Ruby remembered she used to have a lump there. The cotton she had given to me to charge was old stuff she had slept with more than a year earlier.

I immediately trashed that cotton. Now I instruct everyone to discard theirs after about a week's use. That time period is arbitrary, but then so is the duration, the frequency, and the number of my treatments. I have never had an opportunity to establish proper dosage in the lab under controlled conditions. With mice you can play around, but with people I always overtreat because I don't know what's happening, and I have to wait for test results to be sure that a cure has taken place. This is frustrating. Perhaps I could be treating six people in the time it now takes to do one.

Not long ago I found an urgent message on my answering machine from a friend to whom I had sent some charged cotton for the purpose of microscopic analysis. "You gotta call me back right away!" he insisted. "This is important."

Since my friend is usually a reserved guy, I couldn't imagine what had happened, so I returned his call on the spot. Though the microscopic analysis hadn't turned up anything interesting, he had applied the charged cotton to himself. "My arthritis has completely gone!" he shouted into the phone. "I can walk and I can jog and I have clearer mental focus."

At last report, he was looking for some raw-cotton long johns and pajamas for me to charge!

One case involving cotton came with a built-in control. A semi-feral cat that a woman, Irene, was handling raked her throat and chest, leaving multiple gashes about a foot long. After swabbing off the blood with water, she applied some charged cotton to her chest, but not to the minor, inch-long scratch on her palm. Within a couple of hours, the wounds on her chest had turned white, whereas the superficial scratch on her palm had acquired a red scab. A few days later, her throat and chest gashes had completely healed, leaving no marks. The wound on her palm took several weeks to heal, leaving a pink scar still visible a month later.

In a more dramatic case, Janis, who was in her twenties, had been diagnosed with ovarian torsion, which means twisted fallopian tubes, along with cysts, causing the ovarian tissue to die. An operation was scheduled, carrying with it the chance she would become infertile. After I treated her a few times, ending her pain, I gave her a bunch of charged cotton to treat herself.

When Janis went for her pre-op exam, her doctor was astonished: "There are no growths!"

He referred her to a specialist, who was just as puzzled. As he mused aloud while looking at her slides, "You've got growths in this photo, but they're gone in the next one. You've got twisted tubes in this photo, but now they're gone. This doesn't make sense."

According to Janis, she kept repeating, "I went to an energy healer," but the specialist pretended not to to hear her.

I'm still confounded by the refusal of so many people in the medical profession to even look at evidence that suggests they may not have all the answers. At least Janis's doctors canceled her operation.

In another recent case, I treated a young woman from Maine, whom I had never met, for breast cancer using cotton alone. Danielle was slated for a mastectomy, which she had been putting off. After a few treatments with the charged cotton, she was told, "The tumor isn't as big as we thought." Her operation was downgraded to a lumpectomy. A later biopsy showed the cancer had disappeared, along with the need for an operation.

As a footnote to this case, I discovered that I had successfully treated Danielle's mother for breast cancer a few years before. It may be that the detachment required for healing exaggerates my natural instinct for compartmentalization, explaining why I sometimes have so little recall of my clinical work.

One welcome use I have discovered for cotton is its effectiveness in treating myself. I have a weakness in my corneas for which the first symptom is blurry vision, possibly leading to abrasion and detachment. On several occasions when a cornea detached, the pain has been brutal, like having a knife plunged into my eye. Trying to distract myself, the way I do when working hands-on with a patient, proved impossible. On impulse I applied a bunch of charged cotton. The relief was immediate.

On a different occasion, an ophthalmologist diagnosed me with a scratched cornea, for which he applied a big, bug-eyed bandage. He told me that healing would take a couple of weeks. After replacing the bandage with charged cotton, I went back to see him several days later.

He was baffled. "Your cornea has healed."

"I tend to heal quickly."

"No, you don't understand. I can't find any evidence that the accident happened."

I have now become so sensitized to cotton that I can't turn off my hand when in contact with it. It just goes on fire. To see what might be happening, a biologist friend from Washington State set up an experiment with George, a retired railway worker who claimed to see auras. Since George had leukemia, I was to send him batches of charged and uncharged cotton in identical envelopes. He picked the right stuff every time. We couldn't deceive him. He described the envelopes with the charged cotton as "leaking chi."

One of the coolest gifts I have ever received was a big bag of cotton given to me by Grad. It had been energized by Oskar Estebany for use in Grad's pioneer healing experiments. Grad told me I had taken his research to the next level. That's also the coolest compliment I have ever received. The Estebany cotton is more a museum piece than something I might use. I'm hoping to pass it on to another healer some day.

16. Farewell

"The most beautiful thing we can experience is the mysterious. It is the source of all true art and science. He to whom this emotion is a stranger, who can no longer pause to wonder and stand rapt in awe, is as good as dead: his eyes are closed."

—ALBERT EINSTEIN

I COULDN'T HAVE IMAGINED BACK in 1976 when Ben and I had our last confrontation that I would never again see this man who had so profoundly influenced my life. Our separation seemed to be one we both needed, since neither of us made any effort to bridge the gap. I heard, via the upstate New York grapevine, that he had gone to live in some kind of commune. That was all I knew for almost three decades.

About six years ago, chance brought me into contact with Ben's son, Stuart, and he filled in some of those missing years. Shortly after our breakup, Ben had abandoned his family to move in with another woman. That didn't surprise me, since the relationship between him and his wife had always seemed chilly, and I knew that Ben had affairs. However, most of the money on which his family subsisted had come from Ben, so they became destitute. No rent. No heat. No food.

The emotional breach was just as rough. I remember twelve-year-old Stuart at poolside as a happy-go-lucky kid who clearly worshipped his father. His sister, who was several years older, was a shy child who Ben always praised as having a mystical bent. She was even more identified with him as daddy's little girl.

After the shock of finding herself on welfare, Stuart's mother switched into survival mode. Not only did she keep the family together, but she earned an undergraduate degree, boosting her income sufficiently to allow Stuart to become a school psychologist and his sister a social worker. Though I have never been in touch with Ben's grown daughter, Stuart seemed to have come to terms with Ben as a special person who was very flawed. A devoted father and husband, Stuart is a low-key, understated kind of guy, whereas Ben was abrasive and egotistical. Occasionally, Stuart kept the family tradition alive by doing healings and readings, which he has always downplayed.

Some years ago, Ben moved to Las Vegas, where he and his partner lived in a trailer park—in a *double* trailer, as Ben apparently liked to point out. My guess is that he was attracted to the gambling, though I hope not, because he was only marginally better at it than I was. Our basic difference was that he loved games of chance, whereas I hate winning a quarter just as much as I hate losing one.

I had Ben's address and phone number in 2004 when I attended a Society for Scientific Exploration meeting in Las Vegas. Boy, was I conflicted! I was going to see him. I wasn't going to see him, but I'd call him. I wasn't going to call him. Well, maybe I would. Ben had been an authority figure to me. When you go back inside your parents' sphere of influence, no matter how good or bad the relationship, you tend to revert.

Events overwhelmed my decision—or appeared to. SSE conferences are so jam-packed with exciting, stimulating events that it's hard to find time to do anything else. I didn't contact Ben, but I did get in touch with his partner a few months later. She and I arranged a time for me to call him.

I was nervous, and our conversation felt awkward. Ben's once-resonant voice sounded weak and frail, but because he knew I had received his number from Stuart, he immediately launched into a defensive screed justifying his behavior toward his family. Despite being in his mid-eighties, he had not mellowed into some warm and fuzzy grandpa.

As I listened, he rewrote his family history as he had once tried to rewrite ours. I remembered how in one breath he used to boast about my healing accomplishments, only to accuse me in the next of trying to sabotage his new ministry by taking it over as pope. As always, he was a man who could do no wrong, and I found myself mentally shaking my head, thinking, "Thanks for reminding me."

Still, I couldn't help but feel a poignancy for this once-vibrant man who now seemed so sadly diminished. With a sense of fatalism, he told me that he felt old and tired, and that he was having breathing problems—no surprise for a lifelong chain-smoker. When I suggested sending him some cotton to help his respiratory system, he was clearly ambivalent—here was the sidekick offering to heal the master! It wasn't a long conversation, no more than ten minutes. I was glad when it was over, and I felt bad about that. Our once-important relationship seemed to have received its last troubling postscript.

I did send the cotton. Through e-mails with Ben's partner, I learned that he had gone into the hospital shortly after our conversation. My ordinary life took over, and about two weeks later I went to London for a brief holiday. The night before my transatlantic flight home, I couldn't sleep, which was uncharacteristic. When I arrived at the airport I found my plane had been canceled, and I had to take another flight. Once again, I couldn't sleep during the trip back. I arrived home at about 5 p.m., exhausted from having been up for about thirty-six hours. I decided to set my alarm for 7 p.m. for what was to be a power nap. Inadvertently—or advertently—I set it for seven in the morning.

About eleven that night, I jolted up in bed. The room was filled with light, which was what had awakened me. I was reasonably alert because I felt something was wrong. It was the damnedest thing! That light seemed to hover in the middle of the room, and I experienced a powerful sense of presence. Spontaneously, I reached out to the light, startling myself by blurting out, "Ben!" I called his name once again. Suddenly I was filled with an overwhelming sense of love—stronger than anything I had ever experienced before, unbelievable, and certainly different from any feelings I'd had around him. I felt the dissolving of all the antagonism between us.

This, I later learned, was the moment Ben died.

He had gone into a coma while in intensive care. His partner had arrived at his room with my cotton just as he woke up. His immediate response was one of annoyance. "What am I still doing here?" he asked.

His partner told him about the cotton.

"Get that stuff out of the room!" he shouted. "If I touch it I can't leave, and it's time for me to go."

Neither Ben's partner nor Stuart were surprised about my story of Ben and the light. Others also had strange dreams, experiences, or visitations around his passing. Ben seemed to be in touch, through some mysterious alchemy, with forces most of us only glimpse.

It's hard to imagine how my life might have been without him.

17. Looking Back, Looking Forward

"Western civilization is virtually unique in history in its failure to recognize each human being as a subtle energy system in constant relationship to a vast sea of energies in the surrounding cosmos."

—EDWARD MANN, Canadian sociologist and energy-healing historian

I BEGAN MY APPRENTICESHIP IN HEALING by helping Ben treat people who came to him with their afflictions. Ben's inner guides were instinct and pragmaticism—what felt right combined with what worked.

After a few years in the clinical field, curiosity about the principles behind hands-on healing inspired me to turn to the laboratory. During the past thirty-five years, I have continued to switch back and forth from applied science to pure science, with questions from one leading to a search for answers in the other.

I'm now willing to sum up what I have learned in six propositions, listed here in descending order. In other words, I'm *most* certain about the first proposition and *least* certain about the last one.

1. Cancer can be cured using energy healing. Though my findings about humans in the clinical field are anecdotal, they reflect decades spent curing many kinds of cancers, with results often backed by systematic medical testing. From the laboratory, I have experimental proof conducted by trained, skeptical observers in five biological and medical institutions. A fatal injection for cancer is sixty thousand to one hundred thousand cells. In all our experiments, we used at least that maximum. Sometimes we used two hundred thousand cells; sometimes the mice were double injected, and even double injected with double-lethal doses.

2. Once an organism has been energy-cured of cancer, it is immune for life. To my knowledge, which is based on self-reporting, no person I've done healing work with for cancer has had a recurrence. In the lab, this also proved true with mice that were allowed to live a full life span. During experiments in the St. Joseph's biology department, attempts to reinfect cured mice failed. At Terre Haute, implanting tumors from treated mice into untreated mice that had been injected with cancer cells seemed to transfer some kind of immunity: only three out of eight produced tumors. All my research points to an immune response. I will be flabbergasted if the mechanism of healing turns out to be something else.

3. Dose matters. For ethical reasons, I have never experimented with dose when dealing with people, opting instead to overtreat so I'm in alignment with my intention to provide the best possible outcome; however, in the biology lab at Terre Haute, Margaret Moga and I attempted to discover the least amount of treatment that would still be effective. When I treated one batch of twenty-five mice only a couple of times from a distance, a few deaths predictably occurred among those with the largest tumors.

4. The more aggressive the cancer, the faster it remits. When doing healing work with humans, I found that aggressive cancers like blastoma remitted faster than slowly developing ones like prostate cancer. This corresponds with laboratory evidence gained treating mice. Since mice injected with mammary cancer had only a fourteen- to twenty-seven-day lifespan as opposed to forty-five to fifty days for sarcoma, I judge mammary cancer to be the more aggressive. In all my experiments, mammary cancer remitted faster.

5. Cancer remits in bursts. My gross observation both in applying hands-on healing with humans and mice is that periods in which nothing seemed to happen were followed by dramatic change. This appears to be supported by my experiments with geomagnetometers

that were put next to mice cages: 20 to 30 hertz oscillations would suddenly slow, at unpredictable intervals, to 8 to 9 hertz, and then to 1 hertz. Similarly, my EEG experiments showed a sudden anomalous switch to pulsations in the 8 hertz range. Though equating these sudden spikes with healing requires a leap of faith, the findings are suggestive.

6. Some types of energy healing may not be compatible with some conventional medical procedures. When my hands-on treatments for cancer were allowed to run their full course, my only clinical failures occurred with patients who had received radiation or chemotherapy. This supports Ben's and my subjective feeling that the energy systems of such patients had been depleted beyond our ability to restore them to health. My assumption is that hands-on treatments nurture the immune system, in contrast to chemotherapy and radiation, which unavoidably kill healthy cells along with the targeted cancer cells.

Though I caution once again that I have listed these propositions in declining order of certainty, I have no doubt about the first one. Energy healing *is* a reality. As a result, many questions need to be systematically explored with suitable lab facilities, qualified personnel, and stable funding.

Here are a few such questions:

- How many treatments are necessary to produce remission? Is it better to have many short treatments or a few longer ones?

- How do different types of cancer respond to the same treatments?

- If remissions can be produced from a distance, does the rate of remission vary with distance? Some psychic researchers say distance is irrelevant for all psychic phenomena. My clinical experience is consistent with this claim.

- Do multiple healers add to the positive effects of energy treatment? Claims are conflicting.

- If a lab animal with cancer is irradiated, will energy treatments be effective?

- Can the effects of treatment be stored in some materials, then transferred to an organism? If so, what materials work best? In Grad's pioneering work at McGill, he found that healer Oskar Estebany could transfer healing effects to water and cotton. My UConn experiments with water and my clinical work with cotton seem to verify these findings.

- Do some materials block the healing effect? Answering this question might shed light on healing's fundamental properties.

- Can healing energy be detected and measured? Many claims for measurable "subtle energy" have been put forward over the decades, but none have gained general acceptance.

- Can hands-on treatment before cancer occurs create immunity? My guess is that it cannot, because healing energy responds to the current needs of an organism.

- Can immunity be inherited? Can an organism that has been cured pass on resistance to the next and subsequent generations?

- Can blood transplanted from an organism that has remitted produce remissions in an untreated one? If so, can a vaccine be made from this blood that will produce remissions in another? This could be the billion-dollar question!

New York cardiologist Dr. Mehmet Oz has predicted that energy healing, which is basic to the East, will become the cutting edge of Western medicine. As he has also noted: while financial systems and manufacturing are global, medicine remains national and local.

This observation suggests that health care is controlled more by tradition and politics than by scientific data. As more than one doctor has confessed after taking one of my workshops, "If I introduce energy healing into my practice, I could lose my medical license." Tough restrictions govern doctors in New York, whereas in Arizona the field is much more open. How scientific is that?

This top-down lock also limits research. It's far harder for me to get funding, lab space, and experimental animals than it is for researchers who want to test drugs, despite my past successes and the obvious fact that hands-on healing is easier on the animals.

All fields of science—physics, chemistry, biology—fiercely protect their orthodoxies. Any findings that don't fit are deemed not to have happened. In the medical field, this is exacerbated by the grip of the pharmaceutical industry. Fortunately this seems to be weakening due to drug recalls, unforeseen side effects, false claims, and favorable results too obviously tied to drug-company funding.

I am, of course, aware of legitimate problems of acceptance with energy healing. The first hurdle is what I call the "boggle effect." The idea of curing cancer with hands-on healing is just too good to be true. I get that. A physicist friend of mine is working on a system that he says will beat the second law of thermodynamics and produce endless amounts of nonpolluting energy. That boggles *my* mind, but either he can produce the data or he can't. Most of the big discoveries in science turn their fields upside down, but those on the inside usually ignore the anomalies until these can't be ignored any longer.

The same attitude prevails with respect to unusual abilities. If a savant can instantly come up with the square root of a seven-digit number or play a complicated musical composition after hearing it once, that person should be given center stage, not turned into a freaky sideshow. How does he do this amazing thing? Why can't we all do it? Can we find out how this happens in order to apply it? If Ben could heal hands-on, why can't everyone? Can this skill be analyzed and taught to others?

The second obvious problem with energy healing is determining who is qualified to practice. Currently anyone can claim to be a healer, whether through genuine ability, fraud, or self-delusion.

I would like to see the development of tests that can show "something" relevant is happening when healing is supposed to be occurring. For example, after I held a beaker of water for several minutes, a chemist friend reported that the water's oxygenization had increased 25 percent. When he tested other healers, increased oxygenization also occurred, but only by about 1 percent. Does this have anything to do with healing? The field is still too mysterious for us to know.

So many questions . . . Over the next few years, I hope to find some of the answers.

18. Touching the Source

"My own suspicion is that the universe is not only queerer than we suppose, but queerer than we can imagine."

—J. B. S. HALDANE, British geneticist and evolutionary biologist

THREE PSYCHICS HAVE TOLD ME the same thing: "You've touched Source energy." Though I don't know what that means, I sometimes do have an experience of traveling to a place in which everything I need for healing is in infinite supply. My mind moves past my cycling images and the life they describe, into superconsciousness and a sense of higher intelligence, then past that into peace, and past that into Nothingness—a place of pure potential where all possibilities exist at the same time. The higher I go, the less I feel. The Source doesn't do anything. It just is.

The best way I can describe Nothing that contains Everything is through the metaphor of white light. Physicists tell us it contains all other colors: when we see red or green or yellow, that's a subtraction from white. To create his paintings, Picasso subtracted what he needed from white. Subtract another combination and you get a Jackson Pollock or a da Vinci. If you master white, then you have mastered all colors.

Perhaps by touching the Source I can give my patients what they need to heal, because the Source offers an infinite number of simultaneous existences transcending time and space. Perhaps there's a place where you crushed your finger, and a place where you did not; there's a place where the finger heals, and a place where it does not. These places are probably very close to each other, so if we act quickly before your thoughts have had a chance to harden around a negative reality, maybe we can make it back together to the noncrushed-finger time. With negative belief, you're shutting down possibilities that you might not have known existed. I'm trying to open you up to a wider spectrum of alternatives.

With conditions that develop slowly, like some cancers, the task may be to reverse the procedure through a series of existences during which the cancer diminishes into nonexistence. Perhaps this means moving forward in time or perhaps it means moving back, because inside the Source present, past, and future are without distinction.

Consciousness does not have a plural. That may be instinctive wisdom that we have built into the language, reflecting our awareness that all consciousness is connected. When I'm treating you, what I think of as my consciousness and what you think of as yours may be traveling through concurrent existences together. If mine is an experienced traveler, perhaps I can nudge yours into a place where your body would prefer to be—a place where you live and not where you die. You may think I'm changing something physical in you the way a doctor would, but maybe you get better because I take you to the right place, like transporting an asthmatic patient to a climate that ameliorates that condition.

Many people yearn for an elusive sense of wholeness that they fleetingly touch through big experiences, such as birth and death and love, and artistic or scientific invention. Alternatively, such moments may arrive unexpectedly through an event that seems mundane, such as gazing across a beautiful valley, glimpsing an exotic bird through foliage, or watching children at play. Perhaps these moments spring from our intuitive knowledge that we are part of something much larger than ourselves. Perhaps all Creation as we know it is an extraction from a totality, which I have chosen to call the "Source." Just as artistic perfection may mean taking all the great paintings in the world and returning them to white light, perhaps touching the Source destroys Creation at that moment for that person.

Recently I have studied Buddhism, and of course I see the parallels between my ruminations, arrived at innocently and independently, with the Buddhist concept of nirvana. I know a monk who has spent the past twenty years meditating nineteen hours a day, sleeping four, and eating during one. He walks around with a big grin on his face, apparently content and happy, but that's not a life I would choose even if I could achieve it. I like what I know of Creation. I have no desire to devolve it back to Nothing or to absorb all colors into white. I would prefer to understand the workings of the world we now enjoy, which for me often comes down to healing.

Just as I speculate that Creation may be a subtraction from the perfection of Nothingness, I see disease as a subtraction from perfect health. I find that I'm unconsciously drawn to physical need in others, and that somehow I'm able to offer a patient what he or she requires. Instead of time travel backward or forward, perhaps I'm able to access some kind of universal energy, intelligence, awareness, or information beyond my perception. I can't describe any of this more clearly—that's why we have poets!

What I am sure of, through personal experience, is that this kind of healing is a natural system, not a magical one, which is why it's also an imperfect one. Sometimes I can help, and sometimes I can't. What I endeavor to do is to offer patients the whole spectrum—metaphorically, white light—in hopes they can subtract from it what they need in order to return to health. That's different from my healing them, though out of habit I still use that word. It's also why I'm always surprised when patients thank me for restoring them to health. While those were my hands moving around, I never feel as if I was the healer.

Cycling is hard work but touching the Source is not. Think of that other kind of cycling—pedaling a bike to the top of a steep hill, then letting go . . . surrendering. Now you're not doing anything. You're just sailing along for the ride.

But is it really necessary for me to tell you these things? In the national survey I mentioned earlier, 40 percent of all Americans admitted to having had at least one profound mystical experience that took them beyond time and space, with many others perhaps too shy to report such experiences. That was touching the Source. And the Source doesn't pay attention to national borders. In countries where the spiritual is woven more firmly into daily life, the numbers are likely to be much higher.

My hope is that all those who read this book take from it an expanded sense of the resources offered by the Universe, along with a greater awareness of their own potential in calling upon that abundance, not only for healing, but for all aspects of life. The possibilities are infinite. The limitations are our own. Not faith, not belief, but trust.

APPENDIX A

How to Apply Hands-On Healing

Please read the following Disclaimer before proceeding further:

The information presented in this section of the book, entitled "How to Apply Hands-On Healing," is a "supplement" that is educational in nature and is provided only as general information. As part of the information contained in the supplement, you understand you will be introduced to the basics of the energy-healing method the author developed and identifies as the Bengston Energy Healing Method™ (the "Method"). The Method consists of two steps—the first is to create a "list" (as defined on the following pages) and the second is to perform a technique the author calls "cycling" (also defined on the pages that follow) while applying a hands-on healing technique. The Method engages energy fields and systems that are natural to each person and the universe. The premise is, the Method creates changes in the energy or spiritual aspects of the client, which then can manifest in the physical body. So when a qualified and authorized Method practitioner works with a client using the Method, the practitioner is connecting to the energy or spiritual "bodies" of the client—not the physical body. Therefore, when the author uses the words "treatment" or "treat/s," they are used solely in the context of working with the client's energy or spiritual bodies and not the physical body, which is the domain of the medical field and other allied health-care professionals.

You understand there is a distinction between "healing" using the Method and the practice of medicine or any other licensed health-care practice. The author has a PhD in sociology and is not a medical doctor or other licensed health-care professional. The Method is not a substitute for medical or psychological treatment from appropriate professionals; it would be considered "alternative" or "complementary" to the healing arts that are licensed by the states. The author strongly advises you to seek professional advice as appropriate before making any health decision.

You understand the author makes no warranty, guarantee, or prediction regarding any outcome from your using the Method for any particular issue. You agree to assume and accept full responsibility for any and all risks associated with using the information contained herein about the Method. In addition, you understand that learning about the Method in the supplement does not authorize you to represent in any manner that you're a Bengston Energy Healing Method™ practitioner or to use the Method in a professional therapeutic setting. The author accepts no responsibility or liability whatsoever for the use or misuse of the information contained in the supplement. By continuing to read the supplement, you knowingly, voluntarily, and intelligently assume these risks, including any adverse outcome that might result from experiencing the Method and/or using the information contained in the supplement about the Method, and you agree to fully release, indemnify, hold harmless, and defend the author and his heirs, agents, publisher, consultants, and employees from and against any and all claims or liability which you, or your heirs and/or representatives, may have for any loss, damage, or injury of any kind or nature whatsoever arising out of or in connection with reading the supplement and/or using the Method. If any court of law rules that any part of this Disclaimer is invalid, the Disclaimer stands as if those parts were struck out.

The Bengston Energy Healing Method™ is a trademark of the author's and may only be used with permission.

By continuing to read the supplement you agree to the Disclaimer.

CAN HANDS-ON HEALING BE TAUGHT?

"I am convinced that medical science not only has not had the last word, it has hardly had the first word on how the world works, especially where the mind is involved."

—**LARRY DOSSEY, MD,** American internist and author

After my second mouse experiment, I was sure that hands-on healing could be taught. Hadn't I just turned four people, all skeptics, into cancer healers during six weeks of lessons? Later when I discovered resonant bonding, I knew all bets were off. If only one of my recruits could heal, then perhaps he or she had cured all the mice. Even worse for the possibilities of teaching: had I accidentally remote-healed the mice without ever going near their cages?

No one taught Ben. Not only did his talent emerge spontaneously, but he initially wished to get rid of it. Then over the years, he learned through trial and error to develop and control it. Did Ben teach me? Did I acquire my ability through observation and osmosis, or was I drawn to him because I unconsciously knew that I already possessed the talent? What effect, if any, did cycling have on my ability? Could I use this method to teach others? Could they in turn teach it to a new generation of healers?

The theoretical evidence was strong. Hands-on healing has emerged independently as a tradition in most cultures, including the West, despite having been severely repressed for the last three hundred years. If healing is a talent like musical and artistic ability, the statistician in me knows it's reasonable to assume that it is distributed throughout any population on some sort of bell curve. While Mozarts and da Vincis may be rare, every society probably produces significant numbers of inherently talented people who could benefit through schooling, apprenticeship, modeling, encouragement, and guidance. Though it may be impossible ever to determine whether a teacher creates ability or merely attracts it, the result is potentially the same: a group of healers emerges where none was known to exist before.

Who Can Become a Healer?

In tribal societies, the role of shaman was often hereditary, suggesting talent could be inherited. Sometimes apprentices were selected because of a tendency toward seizures—a condition that even today is often connected with paranormal experience. Sometimes these apprentices had to undergo life-threatening ordeals, most likely requiring them to enter a prolonged altered state in order to survive.

In Western culture, Jesus is still the preeminent model of a hands-on healer, suggesting that this ability is the overflow of a wise, compassionate, highly evolved consciousness. Those words could not be used to describe Ben, undeniably a Mozart of healing. He was short-tempered, moody, dictatorial, and very hard on the people closest to him. In fact, his main strength as a healer might have been his galloping arrogance. He was a self-described megalomaniac who believed he was smarter than everyone else. Like a child, he saw himself as without limitation, so if someone else was able to heal, then of course he could do it better. He was never threatened by another person's perceived superiority; nuclear physicist or shoe-shine boy, it was all the same to Ben.

He also had an unusually well-developed ability to get out of the way. His joke—that he was from Alpha Centauri—had its own truth, because it allowed him to distance himself from any real commitment to this world. He was an out-of-towner, a tourist who could observe without tying himself into knots about the outcome of his actions. At the same time, he had a profound and undeniable connection with some kind of wisdom, which I have come to call the Source. He also saw the bigger picture far more clearly and quickly than I did. While I was still wide-eyed about healing, he foresaw the boredom, the rejection, the whole panoply of human contrariness—all things I would have to learn. Whereas Ben defaulted to fate in earthly matters, I always wanted rational explanations.

Analyzing my own qualifications as a healer is far more difficult, because I don't know whether I came by my ability naturally or learned it from Ben. I'm a very good multitasker. I can be very present with a person in one place while simultaneously being somewhere else entirely—an ability reinforced with cycling. When I'm healing, it's almost as if I'm a split personality. You could probably find a diagnosis of my condition in the American Psychiatric Association's manual of mental disorders! I'm also highly motivated. If I commit to something, I'm going to give it all I've got for as long as it takes.

I think it's important for any healer to be caring. While I was in college, which was during the Vietnam War, I kept on my desk that famous picture of the little girl running, after being burned by napalm. I would stare at it, then put my head down, trying to make sense of it. Then I would get up, walk around, and go through the same process all over again. That whole period seemed like madness to me. I have never been able to understand violence or even deliberate meanness. So yes, I believe I'm sensitive to other people, despite having done my share of thoughtless things, and this is probably a useful quality.

When setting up my mice experiments, I consciously selected intelligent skeptics who were motivated to succeed. After the experiments, I gave each volunteer a questionnaire with broad-based queries about lifestyle and experience. No patterns emerged, leaving the field wide open.

Ben was not a miracle worker, and neither am I. Because we were able to effect positive outcomes, some yet-to-be-discovered scientific principle must be involved. Though my body knows how to digest an apple, I don't know how it knows. The same goes for energy healing: I can't tell you how the process works, but I can describe the techniques that emerged from our years of practice. Remember, what I'm giving you here is the equivalent of a musical score. How well each of you can play it is beyond my ability, and probably yours, to predict and control.

Why the List?

The method Ben and I devised was not something that happened on a Monday and was ready for use on the following Wednesday. Over the years I peppered him with questions, hoping to find ways to reproduce his experiences. What was occurring inside his brain when he was healing? What was he feeling with his hands? In between discussions on horse racing, astronomy, and politics and ordering pizza, we evolved what began to look like a process.

Our two-step method came out of our mutual awareness that it was necessary to distract the attention of both healer and patient from interfering in events on the unconscious level, where we believed the real healing took place. The human brain has two halves—one rational, analytic, and linear, the other more intuitive and holistic. While medical doctors are trained to work out of their left brains—analyzing data, making diagnoses, and prescribing drugs—energy healing probably relies more on the function of the nonverbal, intuitive right brain.

In the seventies, mind-body researchers began experimenting with visualization in an attempt to prolong and improve the lives of cancer patients. That suggested to us the use of images—not as a way to ease symptoms, but simply as a method of ego distraction, allowing the energy to produce a full cure.

That was where the list came in. That it should be selfish seemed obvious to Ben and me. If you ask volunteer healers for a wish list, they're likely to include all sorts of altruistic notions about family, friends, and world peace. Ben and I doubted this lack of self-interest could be sustained over time without a buildup of resentment. This isn't cynicism. It's simply an acknowledgment of who we are as a species. Self-sacrifice often carries a very complicated agenda. In our view, healing should be done as a favor to one's self and not to the other person, because it fulfills a need in the healer. We also concluded from the quirkiness of our patients that you couldn't assume you knew what another person wanted, even if it seemed apparent. We chose instead to feed the ego all the things it secretly longed for in order to get it out of the way, much like diverting a guard dog with raw steak till it becomes satiated.

Ben and I decided the list should contain at least twenty items. That number is arbitrary. How many spokes does it take to make a wagon wheel? Enough to keep it spinning! Add more items if you wish, but don't have fewer than twenty. That's to prevent the ego from drifting off into a narcissistic daydream over individual desires. That's not cycling.

Ben and I were always surprised at how much difficulty people often had in coming up with twenty wishes. The usual impulse is to go generic: health, wealth, happy relationships. When you analyze this response, you uncover a desire on the part of the list-maker to control his or her own universe. Also, placing health or wealth on the list implies you lack these things, which means floating a negative idea. That's why we insisted all items be specific, and that the list-maker remove something after receiving it.

Because Ben and I invented the list as a tool for cycling, we were surprised when it began to acquire a life of its own. At least anecdotally, people claimed to be generating what they had wished for in ways that seemed uncanny, implying that reality had followed their conscious desires. One formerly skeptical woman furiously complained to me that she had received almost everything on her list within a month, in coincidental ways that she found unsettling. Here was the same anomalous, angry response we sometimes received after successfully healing someone! Health and empowerment bring responsibility, just as other kinds of talent do. Think what it must be like to wake up every morning as Yo Yo Ma. You have to continuously practice because you can't afford to give a poor performance. That kind of pressure has to be tough. So is the pressure of discovering that you have the power to shape your own reality, if indeed that's true.

At the very least, compiling your list is an exercise in self-awareness. There's often a big difference between what you think you want and what you actually do want. After imagining yourself as CEO of your company, with all the extra travel and responsibility, maybe your current job, with its generous time for family and hobbies, will begin to look pretty good to you. Maybe the flashy red sports car you've always lusted after in advertisements no longer suits your changing self-image or current lifestyle.

A year ago, I put a state-of-the-art, flat-screen HDTV set on my list, but when my brother offered me one at a ridiculously low wholesale price, I didn't buy it. The truth is, I seldom watch TV. I just thought, in some lesser part of my brain, that it would be cool to own one.

Rules for Making the List

- Write down at least twenty things that you don't have and would like, without regard to when or how each might be realized. Add more if you want—there's no upper limit to the number.

- Make each item as specific as possible. You may include material objects, prestigious honors, emotional desires, or the resolution of physical or psychological problems.

- It's okay to wish to become a world tennis champion or to receive a Nobel Peace Prize; however, along with those remote items, be sure to include more attainable ones, like a new computer, as well as those that would be a pleasant surprise, such as a job promotion for which you aren't the front-runner. These more earth-bound items make your list more specific and more real to you.

- Make every item personal to yourself and completely selfish. This isn't the place for altruism or abstractions.

- If you want to involve other people, be sure to ask their permission. Though it isn't necessary for them to practice the technique, acquiring consent must be considered a strict ethical rule. The one exception involves those unable to give permission, such as small children, people in a coma, and animals. Even then, you should acquire the permission of their chief caregivers.

- Translate each item into a visual image that suggests the wish has already been granted. Choose images that are ends and not means. Don't imagine yourself with a pile of money. Instead, visualize the yacht or the condo you would buy if you had the money. Don't think about the bad knee you want healed. Imagine yourself playing tennis or doing something else you couldn't otherwise do. Don't think about ways and means. Seize on each image as if it were already a reality.

- Invest at least five minutes in each image. Enter into it by using all your senses to make it a real and present part of your life. Imprint it onto your brain.

- You may wish to give each image a one-word name in order to engage your verbal brain.

- Once you've compiled the list, regard every item on it as equal. The desire for a new computer is therefore no more or less important than imagining yourself as president of your company or a tennis champion.

- Review your list to be sure that each of these rules has been followed.

- Consider your list dynamic. Redo it at least every week to see that it continues to reflect your current desires and concerns.

- As soon as a wish has been realized, remove it from the list. Otherwise, you're expressing an unconscious fear that you'll lose what you already have. If you stop wanting something, replace it with something you do want.

Cycling

The second step in Ben's and my evolving healing technique came to be something I called "cycling," which means running through the images on the list more and more quickly in order to speed up neural activity.

When I questioned Ben about healing, he often blurted out answers unknown to his conscious mind. For example, when I initially asked if he were inducing the slow alpha-theta brain waves usually associated with altered states, he insisted, "No, no; faster, faster." Though I have recently read that some Buddhist monks and yogis meditate by speeding up rather than slowing down brain activity, that information was virtually unknown in the West during the seventies. Ben and I were flying on blind instinct.

Ben suggested fueling this practice with emotion, which we mutually agreed was an energy—"e-motion," as Wilhelm Reich called it. Again we were following instinct rather than reason.

While any feeling may be judged positive or negative depending on circumstances, we considered emotion to be neutral when used as psychological fuel. Therefore, it didn't matter whether cycling was attached to anger or to joy. Though I personally default to the positive, I have found that most people prefer to cycle during negative emotions as a displacement technique, while reveling in pleasure during positive emotions without wanting to cycle. Since the technique requires you to ride the emotion rather than replace it, this distinction probably breaks down when multitasking becomes more familiar.

How long does it take to learn to cycle? Cycling isn't a place you get to. It's a process. You're never "there." It's like playing tennis: you're always trying to improve. Even if you do become a world champ, you can still up your game unless you're winning every stroke, every match, every day.

Hypercycling came about as a game between Ben and me when we were treating together, with four hands on the patient. If I suddenly speeded up my cycling, Ben would shoot me this knowing look, then throw it back at me. We would challenge each other like in a game of ping-pong, with each of us cycling more and more quickly, till some of our more sensitive patients commented on the increase in the energy flow.

I now consider upping the flow a permanent part of my treatment repertoire, both to increase energy when I need it and to keep myself from becoming bored. When asked how I do this, I reply, "How does anyone decide to walk faster?" You intend it, by sending a message to your brain. However, just as you can't break the four-minute mile without practice, you can't hypercycle by intention alone.

That Ben's brain was speeding up rather than slowing down when in healing mode had been demonstrated decades earlier at the American Society for Psychical Research, though ASPR researchers had attributed those results to machine malfunction. At that time, the highest brain-wave frequencies were thought to be beta (30 hertz). Today, gamma states (40 hertz) have been recorded, as well as hypergamma, lambda, and epsilon, with frequencies close to 200 hertz. In these upper ranges, all brain waves appear to become harmonized. Again this confirms Ben's ASPR tests in which slow and fast waves seemed to register simultaneously—another result blamed on machine malfunction!

Though Ben and I invented cycling as a means to an end, I have come to suspect that it might create long-term, desirable psychological and physiological changes in the brain, just like meditation does. Some cyclers report that it allows for a general lessening of tension and an increased sense of optimism. I have even had therapists and psychiatrists report to me that patients who have learned cycling are more focused and respond better to physical and mental testing.

This, combined with my own experiences with fMRIs and EEGs, has persuaded me that cycling may be a phenomenon well worth investigating apart from my use of it for healing—and that's a realization which, over the years, has taken me by surprise. What I already know is that my own brain is not considered normal, perhaps as the result of cycling. If this is a reproducible effect, maybe everyone who adopts my method is really an alien-in-training!

Rules for Cycling

1. Organize the items on your list in a way that will help you memorize them. For example, group together all those having to do with your home, followed by those involving outdoor activities, work, personal relationships, travel, and so on. Alternatively, you may wish to put the words attached to the images in alphabetical order, or group the items in fives. Use any memory aid you find useful, except for linking them by a story line.

2. Go through the items on your list one by one, visualizing each for a second or two, using your written copy as a prompt.

3. Run through the items until they're so imprinted on your mind that you can review them backward, forward, and at random. Remember to keep them unrelated, which means giving up the memory aids you used as training wheels.

4. Begin by cycling the images one per second, then two per second, continuing to speed up until you are flipping through all twenty in a single second. You may find it useful to drum your fingers to the beat, or use a stopwatch or a metronome.

5. As you speed up, the images become a blur devoid of emotional or sensory content. You may wish to visualize flipping through them like a deck of cards or spinning them around on a filmstrip loop from an imaginary projector. One of my students likes to visualize them swirling on a sideways figure eight, which is neat because that's also the symbol for infinity.

6. Every now and again, let one of the images pop into consciousness to make sure you're still cycling. Because this is a random process, the same image should not keep reappearing. Once you have mechanically acquired the technique, continue to practice whenever you are experiencing an emotion, whether positive or negative—the stronger the better. Don't try to replace the emotion. Think of your feelings as fuel for multitasking. Remember, multitasking is something we humans accomplish all the time. When a child is learning to walk, each step takes conscious effort; however, as adults we walk, talk, breathe, observe, and listen simultaneously without difficulty. At first cycling may require great effort, but the more you practice, the more natural it will become. You'll know you are mastering the technique when you find yourself automatically cycling while experiencing an emotion, without having to prompt yourself. Don't expect this to happen overnight, anymore than you would expect to compete at Wimbledon after a couple of tennis lessons.

7. Hypercycle from time to time to turn up the energy flow. Do this by intention, then get out of the way and let the process take over.

Just You: Cycling Practice

I have discovered that it's often easier for people to cycle if they begin with a meditation. This is like slowing a car to twenty miles an hour, then accelerating to a hundred. Though your brain waves slow down and speed up many times a day, this process is usually unconscious. This exercise helps you to bring these changes into conscious awareness and control in order to harness your brain-power for greater focus and efficiency. A good way to slow the brain is to slow the breath.

1. Sit in a quiet, comfortable place where you won't be disturbed and where a clock with a second hand is in easy view.

2. Inhale to the count of four; hold the breath for four more counts; exhale to the count of four. With practice, you may wish to increase the count to six or eight. Do this for five to ten minutes.

3. Start cycling, at first slowly, then building speed. This is where you'll find the clock's second hand useful. If you find your mind drifting off, just bring it back to the

task at hand without judgment. If you get bored, frustrated, or impatient, use that feeling for cycling.

4. Slow down your cycling from time to time, then speed up into hypercycling. Increase the time you spend cycling just as you would with meditation.

Learning to Feel the Energy

Many Westerners find it hard to believe in the presence of an invisible energy that Western medicine seldom acknowledges. Fortunately, enough of us have become familiar with Eastern practices, such as yoga and acupuncture, to have experienced some of this energy's effects firsthand.

Everything that exists, including ourselves, is composed of energy. This isn't New Age lore, but modern physics. These energy fields affect both our moods and our interactions with those around us. Some of us are sensitive to this energy, while others need training, or permission, in order to experience it.

To feel the energy in your own hands, hold your palms an inch or so apart. Gradually draw them farther away, then closer together again. The closer they come, the more powerfully you will feel their attraction, rather like iron filings attracting to a magnet.

For Two: Hands-On Training with a Partner

By definition, energy healing is an interaction between two organisms. To practice its techniques, you need a partner or a willing volunteer. Or a cat, a dog, or a gerbil. This ten-step exercise is designed for treating with a partner; however, when treating a volunteer who does not wish to learn the technique, simply eliminate the first two steps, in which the two of you explore each other's energy, along with the need for the volunteer to cycle. As an important ethical consideration, remember to always get permission to attempt healing from the person with whom you are working.

1. Stand about a yard apart, facing your partner.

2. Stretch out your palms toward each other. Explore the energy between you by slowly and spontaneously moving your hands around each other. Be sensitive to your partner. Know that energy fields exist all around you and that they are alive. Be playful and confident.

3. The designated patient sits on a stool or low-backed chair while the healer continues to explore the patient's force field from various angles and distances. Do this for about two minutes, with both partners cycling.

4. The healer cups his or her hands around the patient's neck and shoulders and holds them there for ten to fifteen minutes, still attempting to get the "feel" of the patient. The mind-set of both healer and patient should be focused detachment—an oxymoron describing

opposites to be combined in an instinctive or a learned way that defies verbal explanation.

5. The healer attempts to experience the energy flow from her healing hand, through the patient, into her opposite hand, up into her brain, and then around again, creating a circuit. This becomes easier with practice, but don't expect consistent progress. Though I strongly favor my left hand as the dominant healer, some of you may prefer your right hand.

6. Both healer and patient may experience heat coming from the healer's hands. With me, the radiation originates in a spot in my left palm, just off center toward my thumb. Both healer and patient may experience sensations in various parts of the body: the brain (where cycling is taking place), the solar plexus, or the heart.

7. The healer should attempt to step outside the process to objectively self-observe. Self-consciousness gets in the way. So does wondering if you're as good as someone else, or having too much ego invested in the result.

8. Follow your hands, letting them move to other parts of the patient's body, perhaps to the solar plexus or lower abdomen.

9. Feel for heat coming out of some part of the patient's body. This may be quite obvious, like finding a burning candle with your eyes closed. These hot spots indicate places in need of treatment, whether or not they correspond to known disease or injury sites.

10. Treat these spots by placing your hands there.

After completing this exercise, it's appropriate to thank your partner, because the exchange of energies is an intimate interaction. You should also compare notes about the experience. Novice healers are often surprised to learn how completely their "reading" of a stranger's body corresponds with that person's subjective feelings about his or her health.

When treating or being treated, my students usually report tingling, shaking, vibrating, heating; however, I have successfully treated patients and mentored healers who experienced no sensation at all. During my first treatment of one healer, he reported a sharp sensation that shot up his arms into his head; in my second treatment, he experienced nothing whatsoever. I came to suspect that the first treatment righted some energy imbalance between us. By the second, his command of the energy may have been close enough to mine so that no marked imbalance remained to be righted.

While novices find it reassuring to experience big effects, I don't consider their presence an indicator of success. In fact, I have recently found that I sometimes feel nothing during a treatment in which a patient reports an unusually powerful healing. I compare this to the operation of a dimmer switch: when you dim the lights, you're not using less power. Instead, less energy is going into producing light, with the excess wasted as heat around the switch. Take a 100-watt bulb, then dim it to 20 watts, and you're converting 80 watts of the potential light into heat. Perhaps when I'm feeling nothing, it's because energy is being converted more efficiently into healing power. While I also find it more satisfying to experience sensations and to receive feedback from a patient, that's about me and not about healing.

When the above exercise has been completed, healer and patient exchange places and repeat.

For Groups: Increasing Energy Flow

I like to teach groups so that students can practice on a variety of partners. It's also fun to experience the buildup of energy in a room in which several dozen pairs of people are treating each other. This next exercise helps to enhance that experience.

1. Select a leader.

2. Seat yourselves comfortably, then start with a five- or ten-minute meditation. For example, the leader can slowly count the group down a flight of stairs into deep relaxation.

3. The leader signals the group to start cycling by beating a finger on a hard surface, beginning at one beat per second, then gradually building speed over the next five minutes to what sounds like a drumroll.

4. When the leader stops drumming, the group divides into pairs.

5. While facing each other, the partners mutually feel each other's energy, as previously described, for five or ten minutes.

6. From time to time, the leader instructs participants to speed up or slow their cycling.

7. At the next signal, each pair joins up with another pair to create groups of four.

8. The members of the groups feel each other's energy for five or ten minutes, with the leader instructing them, at random intervals, to speed up or slow down.

9. At the next signal, the groups of four form groups of eight, and so on, until everyone is included in a single group. The intensity of the energy usually increases dramatically with increased numbers.

Enjoy a Group Healing

1. Seat yourselves comfortably, then start with a five- or ten-minute meditation as before.

2. The leader signals the start of cycling by beating a finger on a hard surface, at one beat per second, gradually building speed over the next five minutes to what sounds like a drumroll.

3. When the leader stops drumming, the participants assemble into circles of about eight, or into a single circle, depending on the size of the group.

4. As members of the circle continue to cycle, each one takes a turn sitting or standing in the center to become the focus of group energy and healing.

While these exercises may seem simplistic, repetition can create powerful effects, the way a ripple turns into a wave. Mastery is easier in an atmosphere of playful relaxation rather than one of deadly seriousness.

Of course, these training sessions should be followed with repeated practice on friends, relatives, acquaintances—whoever is willing to cooperate.

What Is Attunement?

Some practitioners believe their healing ability can be relayed to others through a process called "attunement." A teacher who possesses a natural talent or has mastered a technique passes it on to a student through person-to-person interaction. It's said that the purpose of this interaction, the details of which are often kept secret, is to establish some sort of energetic, vibrational frequency between master and student. Such an initiation is, for example, basic to the teaching of Reiki.

Quite probably Ben attuned me in some way through our close association as healers. From our clinical experience, we also came to believe that the people we healed acquired a temporary ability to heal others. We guesstimated this effect to last about five to seven days, based on anecdotal evidence: "I went home and I touched my cat. It used to limp and now it doesn't limp anymore," and so on.

Ideally, I would like to treat each student hands-on, then instruct him or her to reproduce that same effect on others, not consciously, but the way one memorizes a successful golf stroke, then tries to repeat that total experience. Some healers believe the attunement process can be kick-started through active intention, which might include attending seminars or reading instructional materials like this appendix.

Groups of healers may also be able to continuously attune and reinforce each other by creating a group frequency. Though that seems plausible to me, this is just speculation on my part.

For Novices: Hands-On Training

As a novice, you may prefer to begin with ailments for which you can receive immediate feedback, such as headaches, nausea, or back pain. Remember, you are not treating the physical body but the energy or spiritual "bodies" of the client with the intention that healing changes in the client will manifest as positive changes in the client's emotions, behaviors, and/or physical body.

Location

Choose a place where you and the patient can relax. Some healers believe in conditioned space, meaning a room they assume holds good energy because they have used it repeatedly for treatment; however, if you can condition a space positively, then you can also condition it negatively. The last place vulnerable people should go is a hospital, because that's where all the superbugs hang out! I feel the same way about setting up a permanent place of treatment, but that's personal to me and probably not practical for many dedicated healers.

Preparation

I don't prepare for a treatment beyond holding the intention to heal. I even let go of that as a conscious thought as soon as the treatment begins. Many self-help books talk about controlling one's life through intention, meaning focused concentration, but intention can also be gentle, and that's the part of the spectrum that engages me.

Atmosphere

If you like music and candles, then go for it, but I'm dead set against any kind of set ritual. Over time these tend to grow more elaborate, becoming an end in themselves and sucking the vitality out of a process that should remain spontaneous. If you always start by hitting your Tibetan bowl and listening to the same chant, you are suggesting that every treatment is the same, but in fact each one is a new adventure. If you go scuba diving today at the same time and place as you did yesterday, you may see the same rock formations, but everything else will be different—the temperature will have changed, along with the currents and the play of light and shadow. Some organisms will have died and others will have been born. You won't find the same fish, and you won't be the same person with the same experiences and feelings as the day before. No matter how many times I treat mammary cancer, each person is unique, and so is each cancer. I may want to end up in the same place as I did last time, with the patient experiencing a positive outcome, but I have no control over how I'm going to get there.

Expectations

As part of your informed-consent process, ask each patient what you can do for him or her. Some of my patients are startled by that question—they think I should know. Some list a bunch of symptoms. Some provide a precise analysis from one or more doctors. What I'm really trying to discover is that person's expectations of me and the treatment.

Position

Ask the patient if he or she is comfortable lying down. I prefer this position for a generic treatment because the places I want to touch are the solar plexus and especially the lower abdomen, both energy centers to which I feel a strong connection. If you're dealing with a stranger, or someone who isn't comfortable with that much intimacy, have him or her sit on a stool or a low-back chair so you can treat the shoulders and neck instead.

Hands On

After receiving permission, place your hands directly on the patient's body. Mammals like to be touched. This brings about relaxation, and it's also the way my method works best. When I have a desire to move my hands rapidly to shake something up, then I'll work a few inches away from the body, because I'm not a masseur. It's important to release your hands to let them travel instinctively and spontaneously. Don't let a patient tell you where to place them.

This is an unconscious process. The patient's consciousness doesn't know the answers anymore than yours does.

Sensory Clues

Feel around the patient's body for hot spots. It's common among healers of different schools to consider these to be places in need of healing. Trust your hands even when the locations to which they are drawn don't correspond to a patient's reported areas of pain or disease. When I feel a beam of heat coming from a person's body, I'll connect the beam in my left palm to their beam, matching heat to heat. Sometimes I'll feel a strong desire to move my hands even a quarter of an inch. It's as if a request comes up from the patient's body, grabs my hand, and pulls it down.

While treating an autistic twelve-year-old boy, I was surprised by the certainty with which my hand zoomed to a spot on the top of his head. With a forty-year-old woman who had osteoporosis, my hand went to her coccyx (tailbone) and then her neck, even though her whole spine had degenerated.

From time to time, I may have a strong desire to up the energy flow. I have one patient who's so sensitive she picks up the change even as I form the intention. Though I would swear I haven't moved a muscle, she asks me, "What did you do just then?"

Sometimes my hands actually seem to enter a patient's body to fix something. Tumors feel like hard, foreign tissue even when they're out of reach. As I treat them, they soften and grow more pliable till they feel like healthy flesh.

Don't be discouraged if you fail to pick up sensory clues. While they may reassure you that something is happening, they aren't essential. Perhaps with experience you'll begin to feel them. Perhaps not. What's important is the effect of your treatment on the patient, not how it affects you.

Cycling

Novices to my method often find it difficult to remember to cycle. It's natural to have to remind yourself from time to time. When that happens, just pick up where you left off, without self-censure. If you are sincere about the practice, you will find it becoming more natural. By now cycling is so familiar to me that I become aware of it only when confronted with something that makes me nervous.

Letting Go

As I have said many times, normal waking consciousness is an impediment to healing. This even includes holding too strongly the intent to heal. Let that go as well. Remember, you are just a conduit for the energy.

Sometimes when I'm working hands-on, all boundaries dissolve and I can't distinguish between the patient and myself. Though I know from my lab experiments that these special periods produce waves of coherence on a geomagnetometer, I still don't know if that's when healing occurs. It would be gratifying to me if that were so, but once again, that's about me.

You may be someone who finds it easy to go into an altered state. If so, that may be part of the payoff for you. At the same time that you're learning about the patient, you're also learning about yourself. Each healer is as unique as each patient.

Emotion

Cycling is a useful tool for dealing with the boredom that can result from standing for an hour with your hands on someone. After all, boredom is an emotion, too. Same with resentment or any other negative feeling that may arise from the interaction between yourself and a patient. I'm most annoyed by those who keep asking, "How long will this take? How many more treatments?" as if I'm a nuisance they are forced to endure. Remember, emotion is neutral energy, like the current you get when you plug in a toaster. At the same time, treating means rising above personal reactions to a higher level where all is peaceful and healing can take place.

Diversions

Conversation between you and your patient during a treatment is as optional as a conversation with a taxi driver. Since I don't want my patients focused on their ailments, I sometimes chat to divert them. If someone is expecting an intense dialogue about his or her medical problems, this may cause that person to feel cheated. They think, "Why are we talking about these stupid things? I'm sick. This should be about me!" As with any personal interaction, you should be sensitive to signals.

Duration

Though my treatments are usually an hour long, you may wish to begin with only half an hour. As you gain experience, you will find what works best for you, but don't expect one size to fit all. Occasionally my hand will turn off after a few minutes. I don't mean that I have encountered some malfunction: I mean that what needs to happen in the session has already happened. Usually I'll continue to treat to fulfill the patient's expectations, especially if he or she has traveled a long distance to see me, but that's diplomacy, not healing. On other occasions my hand might get very hot—something internal and deep that I alone can feel. That's another signal that the treatment is over, despite what the clock says.

Disconnecting

After I have finished a treatment, I often have an impulse to rinse my hands with cold water, meaning, "I'm disconnected, I'm done, it's over." This seems to be a common reaction among healers; however, if I ever find myself compelled to do that, I'll stop before it becomes a ritual.

The Continuing Healer-Patient Relationship

If a disease is life-threatening, I may treat someone multiple times in a day. For most other problems, I have the subjective sense that every five to seven days is optimal; however, when patients are "geographically undesirable," I'll treat them every day for as long as they are in my area. Often initial improvement will be followed by one or two treatments when nothing seems to happen. Then suddenly the patient's condition will undergo another positive spurt. I try to keep emotions low-key. If someone gives me terrific news, I say, "Oh, that's good to hear." If someone gives me bad news, I say, "Okay, let's do it again and see what happens."

Sometimes novices surprise themselves with early success, akin to beginner's luck. They attribute this to having mastered a method—"Oh, I've got it!"—only to discover later on that they haven't got "it" at all. Their early successes were due to their openness and their lack of expectation, which they lost when they let consciousness take over. I personally don't think of myself as a healer, though I accept that label for the sake of convenience. Some innocent part of me is always surprised when a sick person gets better, because I'm not the one who has done anything. I'm the conduit, not the Source.

While wishing to help others is an admirable trait, it's a mistake to become too wrapped up in a patient or a situation. You shouldn't be doing all the planning, all the traveling, all the sacrificing, unless a patient is comatose.

Even then, make sure you have the permission of the patient's chief caregiver.

Guard against becoming too attached to an outcome. Don't let the desire to help morph into a demand for validation of your own abilities. Just as it's not your fault if a patient dies, it's not your fault if the patient gets cured.

I still haven't solved the riddle of why some people don't return to treatment, especially since this behavior doesn't seem result based. Didn't they want to get better? Did I unconsciously push them away because I couldn't do anything more for them? Did I set in motion a process resulting in cure? Did they die? I'm frustrated, because our relationship ended without my having learned anything.

Resign yourself to the fact that not all people who seek treatment want to get better. Some go through the motions to please others or even to convince themselves. This is also a reality throughout the medical and therapeutic professions, and not just a peculiarity of energy healing.

I consider a treatment to be finished when standard medical tests indicate a condition has been cured or through the patient's self-reporting: "The pain is gone," or, "I didn't used to be able to walk but now I can run."

Sometimes treatments seem to peak, then establish a plateau. That's when a patient is likely to decide, on pragmatic grounds, that it's time to end them. Perhaps if I had treated him or her longer, we would have established a higher plateau. Perhaps not.

When animals and children are cured, you'll find that they just won't be interested in you anymore.

I rarely do follow-ups, though often patients report back to me or signal their satisfaction by referring others.

Given this world's amount of illness and pain clamoring for resolution, every healer needs to maintain boundaries. I know that whenever I go out to dinner with friends, I could instead be healing a person who's sick, but at that moment I want to be with my friends. Doctors face these decisions all the time, which is why they have established clinics and hospitals. Since science doesn't yet understand the mechanism behind energy healing, those of us who have found we can heal are still trying to figure out how to teach others. I have a vested interest in wanting you to learn and then attract students of your own.

What Makes for the Best Prognosis?
These are a few of my personal green lights and red flags:

- A youthful, basically healthy person is easier to treat than an older person with multiple conditions.

- My treatment resonates best with cancer, especially an aggressive one; however, I don't find myself able to counter the damage that radiation and chemotherapy have done to a patient's natural energy and immune systems. You may discover otherwise. I hope you do.

- Injuries are best treated when fresh, before the mind hardens around the idea of being injured or disabled.

- The longer a condition takes to develop, the longer and harder it is to cure. With conditions like arthritis, lessening symptoms is often the best that I can achieve.

- When applying my energy-healing method for addictions or psychological problems, I insist that the patient actively participates by cycling, because we are dealing with a lifestyle change.

- Possessing a close bond with a patient increases the effectiveness of any treatment. Being detached from the process and its outcome doesn't mean being without caring or empathy—yet another paradox.

- A skeptical, open-minded person is most likely to have a successful outcome. Too much belief in myself as a healer or in miracles only gets in the way. Magical thinkers often expect an instant cure. If that doesn't happen, they think they haven't prayed enough or believed enough, putting themselves into a terrible cycle of ups and downs, with any good or bad result becoming exaggerated as if it foretells the final outcome.

- A person who's dying to prove me wrong—sometimes literally—is also a poor patient. Debunkers are strong believers, too; it's just that they believe in something different.

- Patients who are frantically trying everything—vitamins, acupuncture, naturopathy, drugs—also raise a red flag for me. While I understand their desperation, trying everything often means committing to nothing.

- I can smell death, and I don't know how to explain it any better than that. I think other people might be able to smell it, too, if they let themselves. Once someone is in the process of dying, I don't consider it appropriate to interfere. That's why Ben didn't want the energized cotton I had sent to him.

I remember being in a hospital room with an elderly man who had just had his third heart attack. I knew he was dying and he was supposed to be comatose, but suddenly he reached out and grabbed my hand. I could actually feel the energy streaming out of it as if in response to his raw need. He probably lingered about a week longer than he should have because of that contact. I didn't do him any favors.

On another occasion, I decided to treat a control mouse that was a few minutes from death. I worked at it with great intensity, giving it all I had, trying to pull a Lazarus. I was on an ego trip, and the mouse died anyway.

What makes energy healing interesting to me is that it's full of paradoxes and apparent contradictions. Someone who has been diagnosed with terminal cancer may be very ill, but that doesn't mean they're dying. Healing is as much an art as it is a science, with many judgment calls.

Reaching for the Remote

Though I prefer to treat hands-on, I often give charged cotton to people who live at a distance for use between treatments, or even exclusively. For reasons I don't yet understand, I find I can charge it most effectively by holding it between my palms while pacing or just walking around. Even moving my hands when holding the cotton seems to speed up the process of generating heat in a way that has nothing to do with friction.

I usually treat a batch for half an hour, then mail it in plastic, which seems to hold in the energy. I suggest people throw it out after using it for a week, or after they have experienced a major health improvement. As I have demonstrated, you can negatively condition cotton just as you can positively charge it.

If you wish to try treating cotton, make sure it's 100 percent pure, and not the synthetic material available in some drugstores that's rolled and packaged in the same way. Walk around with it between your palms while cycling. Once again, don't think about it consciously; just let the energy do the work for you. Store it in a plastic bag, and experiment with it whenever you have an ache or an injury that needs healing.

Sometimes my students charge cotton as a group. Either they unroll it into a strip so everyone can lay their hands on it, or they stretch it around a circle. When they're finished cycling and charging, they divide the cotton among themselves.

Students also like to bring pictures of those needing a healing to a group practice session. Sometimes these are passed around and sometimes they're placed in a circle for a group healing.

When remote healing with a picture or a hair sample, I also find the treatment is stronger when I move around. Conversely, I'm most effective when I take the picture to bed and sleep on it. Unfortunately, the next morning I'm drained, as if something took over while my guard was down. I do this only if a case is acute and if I don't need the next day myself for something important—another reminder that personal boundaries are essential.

Suggestions for the Practitioner

It's gratifying to me when others who practice energy healing tell me that my method has increased their abilities. For all practitioners, I offer the following suggestions:

1. Find out the legalities governing alternative medicine in your area.

2. Request that each patient sign a consent form in which no claims or promises are made.

3. Urge everyone who comes to you to see a doctor to be tested, diagnosed, and treated.

4. When radiation or chemotherapy has been recommended by the medical profession, explain to the patient that energy healing may not be compatible with those procedures.

5. Do not attempt to influence anyone to take your treatment over the medically prescribed one. What you offer is an alternative, should the patient choose it.

6. If money is involved, it's advisable to accept payment in the form of a suggested donation.

Calling on Helpers

Though I'm not faith based, I understand that looking to a higher power may help some healers get their egos out of the way; however, faith usually comes with a lot of dogmatic baggage, and I hate it when sick people are made to feel that any failure of treatment has to do with some perceived spiritual shortcoming, as if they didn't believe hard enough. Because I consider what I do as a healer to be scientifically based, I dislike having it tied to any belief system. I'm also put off by spiritual bargaining: "If you cure me, I'll build you a chapel and pray four hours a day."

Some healers claim to possess spirit guides through which they channel wisdom and healing powers. Perhaps it's time I confess that even Ben had a group of spirits who followed him around and whom others, besides me, independently could see. They were stereotypically humanoid in shape, without facial features, hands, or legs, as if they were wearing diaphanous sheets too opaque to see through.

When Ben and I went into the apartment of one Manhattan medium, she freaked out: "My God, there's seven of them!" That was the most we ever experienced at one time. On another occasion, I was traveling down a path with a companion when we saw what the paranormal literature calls "floating ectoplasm." She screamed and wanted to run, but I assured her, "It's just one of the Fellows."

That's what Ben called them. We never got into mythologizing them with names or different personalities like Dopey, Sneezy, and Grumpy. If Ben wanted to ask them for help, he did. It was just something he took for granted. They were a presence, like you or anyone else might be.

The Fellows sometimes followed me when Ben wasn't around. I never heard voices or had any sense they were listening or otherwise interacting with me, but I could feel them, and I could see lights and flying sparks.

So here's my dirty little secret. Occasionally—say, once a year if I'm feeling nervous—I'll call upon them: "Hey,

guys, here's something I need." I did that the day I lectured to a crowd of skeptical medical researchers at the
University of Connecticut's Center for Immunotherapy
of Cancer and Infectious Disease. I had no idea where
this engagement might be taking me, so while I was being
introduced I said to the Fellows, "Let's do the right thing
here!" It was a reflex action—an almost comic instance in
which I asked for help without judging what the outcome
should be. Though afterward I received a standing ovation
from the crowd, when I look back at all the disappointment I later experienced at UConn, I'm not sure the right
thing did happen. Maybe the Fellows have a weird sense
of humor. If I were faith based I would say they possessed
some grand design for me that needed UConn to bring it
to pass.

"Fellows" is a generic term. It doesn't mean friends.
The first time Ben mentioned them, I knew exactly what
he was talking about, which doesn't mean they had any
objective reality. We might just have been two delusional
people seeing our version of pink elephants. I do believe
that accessible forces exist outside the self—energy, intelligence, information, awareness—which the Fellows may
engender. Addressing them is the closest I come to prayer.
Instead of calling on a personal God, I'm calling upon
the personal Fellows because at least I've seen them! They
don't come when I call. I don't have a little button I press
to summon them. Maybe I'm just talking to myself, giving

myself instructions. That's okay, too. I don't spend any time thinking about this. It doesn't matter to me.

A Work in Progress . . .

Both in the lab and when I'm healing or teaching, I'm always learning. Understanding and improving my method is an ongoing process that I'm passionate about. I'll come across a new sensation or a new insight, and I'll make changes. Nothing I say or do is fixed for myself or for anyone else.

In attempting to teach others, I'm only offering guidelines to help you find a method unique to yourself, based on your own firsthand experience, internal and external. Most importantly, don't take on my limitations. Just because I can't cure warts or colds or people who have undergone various kinds of radical medical interventions, don't assume that you can't either. Do not put your faith in me. I don't want to be believed. Remember, I'm a faithless person who relies on experience and data. You are part of my experiment. Take what you need from this book, and then go and do it your way, so if I get lost under a bus somewhere it's not going to affect your abilities.

Be better than I am. That's your mandate.

APPENDIX B

Research Guide

"If the attitude of quantum physics is correct . . . then there is no substantive physical world in the usual sense of this term. The conclusion here is not the weak conclusion that there may not be a substantive physical world but rather that there definitely is not a physical world."

—HENRY STAPP, American physicist

THIS SUPPLEMENT IS INTENDED TO provide a brief overview of some of the subjects in this book. It is not intended to be scholarly or comprehensive, but rather it seeks to give the reader some historical sense of selected research that has gone before.

For those of you who are data oriented, there are now many peer-reviewed journals devoted to the investigation of the kinds of phenomena reported here. The most comprehensive is probably the *Journal of Scientific Exploration*, the publishing arm of the Society for Scientific Exploration, which features articles in a wide variety of areas usually labeled "anomalous." For readers more specifically focused on healing, I recommend the *Journal of Alternative and Comprehensive Medicine* and *Explore: The Journal of Science and Healing.*

These three journals are only the tip of a burgeoning movement within science to finally investigate areas traditionally closed off. Such journals, now too numerous to mention, did not spring up overnight, but rather rest on the research of pioneering individuals who bucked the system to go their own way, oftentimes enduring the scorn of their peers. These include, but are not limited to, York Dobyns, Dean Radin, Roger Nelson, Peter Sturrock, Robert Jahn, Brenda Dunne, and all the prominent members of the SSE.

Proving the Principles

Despite Western medicine's rejection of hands-on healing, its underlying principles have been validated in experiments across a wide spectrum of scientific disciplines. These include evidence for the existence of subtle bioenergy fields around living organisms; the ability of conscious intention to influence those fields, and the significance of emotion in heightening effects; the existence of information fields influencing behavior within a species, including the human species; proof that focused intention in the brain of a sender can affect the brain of a receiver; and proof that conscious intention can create physical effects regardless of time and distance.

Communicating with Machines

In conventional science, with its strong materialistic bias, consciousness is considered the spoiler. Whenever it shows up in an experiment, the results are judged to be contaminated because they are subjective rather than objective. However, in recent years this antagonism toward consciousness in the laboratory has come under attack in many disciplines.

One of the founders of the SSE was aerospace physicist Robert Jahn, dean emeritus of Princeton University's School of Engineering and Applied Science, and a member of NASA's Space Science and Technology Advisory Committee. Jahn was lured into anomalous research through a student project, which seemed to prove that humans could, by intention alone, affect the operation of random-event generators (REGs).

An REG is like a high-speed electronic coin-flipper. Instead of heads and tails, it produces pulses that are converted into 1s and 0s—the language of computers. To test the effects of consciousness on the machine, a human subject attempts to influence the REG to produce more heads or tails than the law of statistics allows. With small samplings, any deviation would be meaningless. However, when the "coin" is flipped two hundred times per second, resulting in millions of responses, even a small deviation from randomness to coherence becomes statistically significant.

That's what happened with the student project. On the assumption that this positive data must be due to a design error, Jahn kept tightening the protocols to make them foolproof. Nothing changed. The experiments continued to produce a small but replicable and statistically significant correlation between the human operator's intention and the generator's output.

Eventually the student graduated, leaving Jahn with these intriguing findings—a classic case of "Gotcha!" Despite being one of America's top rocket scientists, he relentlessly followed the controversial data by creating the Princeton Engineering Anomalies Research (PEAR) lab. During PEAR's twenty-nine years of operation, Jahn and his lab director Brenda Dunne, along with a host of incredibly talented researchers, produced an immense database of supporting evidence.

In one benchmark twelve-year study, more than one hundred operators participated in fifteen hundred experimental series, resulting in more than one million trials, employing four kinds of REGs under several distinct protocols. The positive data supporting human-machine interaction remained consistent when the volunteers were thousands of miles from the REGs, eliminating distance as a factor. This consistency persisted even when the volunteers exerted their influence before the machines were turned on. A more startling finding, demonstrated in some eighty-seven thousand experiments, was that volunteers could, through intention alone, affect the findings three days to two weeks after the machines had performed.

In fact, these experiments were even more successful. Not only was the future fluid, but also the past!

Human participants often reported a sense of becoming one, or bonding, with their machines. Pairs of operators with an emotional bond dramatically increased the positive results as much as sevenfold. It wasn't just

Albert + Betty = 2,

but

Albert + Betty = 2++++++

Between 1976 and 1999, the PEAR lab also produced an extensive body of data supporting remote viewing.[1] In 653 experiments, using incisive analytical techniques, researchers produced data confirming the ability of humans to give and receive information-at-a-distance, with a probability against chance of approximately three in ten billion. To achieve positive results, the sender and receiver did not need to coordinate their efforts in time (just as Dave Krinsley and I discovered when we inadvertently sent and received information three hours apart). Something nonphysical seemed to be happening that connected consciousness over both space and time.

In other experiments with REGs, California psychiatrist Richard Blasband demonstrated the effect of emotion on REGs. In 1993, he placed an REG in his office at a distance of ten feet, during a total of thirty-nine therapeutic sessions with eight volunteer patients. The sessions were also videotaped by an unobtrusively placed camcorder to provide synchronized feedback. Analysis of the combined data indicated that the REG distinguished three psychological states: neutral when patient and psychiatrist were merely talking; a greatly elevated REG output resulting in an upward shift on a graph when a patient was angry or elated; and a lowered output creating a downward shift when a patient was crying, anxious, or depressed.

In both the PEAR lab and Blasband experiments, human intent or emotion was the paramount cause of measurable, replicable physical effects. Researchers theorized that an unexplainable resonance between humans and machines had been demonstrated. Through their millions of experiments, PEAR researchers were led to the conclusion that any definition of reality must include the influence of consciousness as an active agent, at least on an equal footing with the senses.

Communicating with Plants

In 1973, the bestseller *The Secret Life of Plants* documented experiments in which Cleve Backster, a leading U.S. lie-detector expert, demonstrated that plants were affected by human intention.[2] In 1966, Backster had accidentally discovered that his polygraph equipment seemed to be measuring the reaction of the plants in his office to his thoughts and feelings. To test this observation, he decided to threaten the plants by burning a leaf to which he had attached an electrode. The moment he formed that thought, his polygraph's recording pen registered extreme alarm.

In later experiments, Backster discovered that distance did not affect his plants' apparent abilities. They picked up his intentions toward them, as their chief caregiver, even when he was hundreds of miles away. To eliminate affecting the plants by his own thoughts, Backster set up an apparatus that randomly dropped live brine shrimp into boiling water when he was not in his office. Again his electroded plants attached to polygraphs registered a sharp reaction the instant each shrimp hit the boiling water. From this and other experiments, he concluded that his plants were in constant communication with all the organisms around them.

Though Backster's findings were replicated by other researchers, he was predictably ridiculed by the scientific community—an insult reflected in his being singled out for one of *Esquire* magazine's 1975 Dubious Achievement Awards: "Scientist claims yogurt talks to itself."[3] At least *Esquire* had called Backster a scientist, which other critics refused to do, despite his use of standard laboratory protocols.

About the same time as Backster was experimenting with plants and polygraphs, chemist Robert Miller successfully demonstrated how intention-at-a-distance can affect plant growth. For this he utilized the volunteer services of aircraft engineer Ambrose Worrall and Worrall's wife, Olga, both famed psychic healers.

On the evening of January 4, 1967, Miller instructed the Worralls to hold in their thoughts some ryegrass seedlings during their usual nine o'clock prayer session. The seedlings were locked inside Miller's Atlanta laboratory while the Worralls were in Baltimore, some six hundred miles away. For several hours before the experiment, an electromechanical transducer had registered stable growth of the seedlings at 6.25 thousands of an inch per hour. At exactly nine o'clock, the seedlings' growth began to accelerate. By morning, their growth registered 52.5 thousands of an inch per hour—an increase of 840 percent! When the Worralls were asked how they had accomplished this feat, they said they had visualized the plants as overflowing with light and energy.[4]

Biological Information Fields

As both Popp (page 184) and Backster demonstrated, the organisms they researched were in constant communication with other organisms by means of subtle and sophisticated systems that on the human level would be called "telepathy" or "ESP."

The idea of information fields, group minds, or a collective unconscious among species has existed on the fringes of biology ever since Darwin introduced his theory of evolution, which was based entirely on mechanistic principles. As evolution's cofounder, naturalist Alfred Russel Wallace, protested: "Material causes alone could not account for the origin of life, the origin of a new species, the creation of human consciousness, or the beginnings of culture." To bridge these gaps in evolutionary theory, Wallace postulated some "driving, shaping, guiding, designing, or willing force" that could come only from the "unseen universe of spirit."[5] While Darwin easily won the nineteenth-century debate, throughout the ensuing decades opposition has collected around Wallace's sense that mechanistic Darwinism is an incomplete system.

In 1953, British biologist Sir Alister Hardy put forth a paper, "Biology and Psychical Research," in which he suggested that animals might share evolutionary information vital for their development through a group mind that he described as "a sort of psychic blueprint between members of a species." Hardy also speculated that all species might be linked in a cosmic mind, capable of carrying evolutionary information through space and time.[6]

Evidence for this group mind is particularly striking among insects, as many researchers have independently discovered. With bees and ants, the actions of the individuals are so well coordinated within the group that many scientists refer to them collectively as "superorganisms." Colonies of harvester ants build radiating roads to food sites half a mile away, and when a road becomes blocked, police ants arrive in a phalanx to construct a detour. Experiments using a stopwatch have verified that these ants appear on-site before an alarm could be relayed by any known sensory or chemical means.[7]

To hide from predators, clouds of tiny coral and green flattid bugs arrange themselves on twigs to look like a single flower with a green tip. When disturbed, the colony instantly reassembles like a well-drilled flash-card routine. How do individual insects learn this trick of coordination? How do they manage to transmit their learning from generation to generation so that the right number of precisely shaded insects—some half-pink and some half-green—continue to reproduce?[8]

British biologist Rupert Sheldrake has attempted to account for these phenomena through his morphogenetic field theory, presented in *A New Science of Life*, published in 1987.[9] According to Sheldrake, each member of a species inherits an invisible information field (or memory bank or blueprint) specific to its own species, along with its DNA. This memory bank directs the development of the embryo using DNA as physical building-blocks. It also continues to guide the behavior of the organism throughout its life by absorbing and circulating the experience of all members of the species, past and present. Therefore, the more members of a species that learn to do something, the quicker all other members will be able to learn the same task, until eventually it may become genetically fixed.

In the 1920s, psychologist William McDougall of Harvard University exposed thirty-two generations of white rats to a water tank with two escape gangways. The gangway that was brightly illuminated produced an electric shock, while the unlit one was safe. Since he kept changing these about, learning occurred when a rat discovered that illumination always meant shock.

Though it took some first-generation rats 330 immersions, the last learned nearly 90 percent faster. However, he noted "the disturbing fact" that control rats from genetically unrelated stock also upped their learning speeds. When McDougall's experiments were repeated by F. A. E. Crew of the University of Edinburgh, Crew's first-generation rats began with the average scores McDougall's rats had achieved after thirty generations, with some rats performing perfectly without a single shock.

According to Sheldrake, unrelated rats were able to learn a skill with increasing speed simply because other rats had previously done so—an ability each inherited through its morphogenetic field. Sheldrake calls this "morphic resonance."[10]

My theory of resonant bonding also suggests that bonded organisms have ways of sharing information regardless of distance—as if plucking information from the air—resulting in observable physical effects. Like morphic resonance, this helps explain McDougall's "disturbing fact" that his control rats seemed to learn at the same time as his experimental ones. Resonant bonding differs from morphic resonance in that it is not species specific. In my experiments, some but not all of the control mice were able to share in the hands-on treatment offered to the experimental mice. Was human consciousness, in the form of intention and empathy, the trump card selectively bonding one group of mice from which others were excluded?

Human Group Behavior

I chose sociology over psychology as a career because I believe psychology, with its overemphasis on the individual, is reductionist sociology. What fascinated me then, and still does, are the social patterns that indicate larger forces at work on human behavior.

Émile Durkheim (1858–1917) is often called the "father of sociology" because he studied the processes holding a society together and those causing it to crumble. In his book *Suicide*,[11] published in 1897, Durkheim demonstrated that suicide patterns in societies were astonishingly regular, which is an observation that holds true today. If you track U.S. suicides by state, you'll find that Nevada will have three times more deaths per hundred thousand than New Jersey, year after year. You can put in suicide hotlines, take them out, flood the state with psychiatrists, collect the data during peace or war, and it doesn't seem to matter.[12]

The implications of this can appear quite bizarre. If you find Jonathan standing on a ledge in a hotel in Nevada and you talk him down, have you saved a life, or does this mean you've just killed Fred because now *he* has to jump to make up the state's annual quota? Most of us reject this view because we prefer to see ourselves acting as individuals rather than as part of a collective. Nevertheless, all human behavior is about interactions. There is no such thing as an isolated individual, unless you were born without parents and never met anybody. If you put two people together, they create a new social entity that is not just the sum of both of them. To use a chemical analogy: if you know everything about hydrogen and everything about oxygen, you still don't know anything about water, which is what you get when you put the two together.

Durkheim applied that same logic to crime, which he considered a normal and even functional part of society because it reinforced social order among non-offenders. The statistics for crime also remain surprisingly stable, with cities having consistently high-crime and low-crime neighborhoods. Immigrants will typically settle in the high-crime, transitional areas because that's all they can afford. Let's say they're Italian. As an ethnic group, Italians will then be blamed for the high crime rate. When another wave of immigrants moves in—perhaps Puerto Ricans—then the Italians will move into more established neighborhoods, where they will integrate without boosting the crime rate. Now the high crime rate in the transitional area will be blamed on Puerto Ricans.

Crime isn't a function of one ethnic group or another, or even of conditions that can be easily measured, like low income. Take, for example, Phoenix, Arizona. When you get off the plane, having just left the slush and gloom of a New York winter's day, the sun will be shining and everyone will be smiling, but Phoenix's crime rate is out of control because no one lives in Phoenix. It's a transitional zone in which everyone is just passing through on the way to somewhere else—a circumstance that benefits no one but the real-estate agents. It's the same with Nevada, which has a high crime rate as well as a high suicide rate. That's because Nevada is to states what Phoenix is to cities—a transitional zone with little sense of community.

These are the effects of Durkheim's laws of social order. Because of his groundbreaking work, it's now standard for sociologists to think in terms of social patterns.

Measuring Brain Activity

In a 2005 study conducted by researchers from Bastyr University and the University of Washington, EEGs and MRIs were used to see if any correlation could be found between the brain activities of bonded human pairs. When the brains of senders were stimulated, the brains of their receiving partners showed the same brain activity, as if they were seeing the same images.[13]

In a previous EEG study, neurophysiologist Jacobo Grinberg-Zylberbaum of Mexico City discovered that participants with the most-ordered brain patterns were likely to lead their partners into synchronized brain activity, but only if they had previously bonded. In similar studies, it was found that the response of the receiver often anticipated the activity of the sender. These results, cited in *The Intention Experiment* (2007), by medical journalist Lynne McTaggart, confirm EEG and fMRI experiments in which I affected the brain waves of volunteer receivers when in healing mode.[14]

In summing up the importance of brain coherence, McTaggart stated, "As one scientist put it, coherence is like comparing the photons of a single 60-watt lightbulb to the sun. Ordinarily, light is extraordinarily inefficient. The intensity of light from a bulb is only about 1 watt per square centimeter of light. . . . But if you could get all the photons of this one small lightbulb to become coherent and reso-nate in harmony with each other, the energy density of the single lightbulb would be thousands of millions of times higher than that of the surface of the sun."[15]

My own sense of being able, at intervals, to access an outside power source was also confirmed by physicist Elmer Green, who found that when healers are focused, they exude electrostatic energy, with one producing surges one hun-dred thousand times higher than normal. He also observed that the pulsations were coming from the abdomen.[16]

Energy Healing

Throughout this book, I have mentioned Bernard Grad's innovative experiments in energy healing. Elisabeth Targ, another colleague with whom I planned to do research before her untimely death, also made a significant contribution to this field. As a psychiatrist at Pacific Medical Center in San Francisco, Targ designed a 1999 double-blind study in which experienced healers from across America sent healing thoughts to terminal AIDS patients whom they had never seen. Each healer received only the name, photo, and T-cell count of a patient to be treated. The healer's instruction was to spend an hour a day for six days sending a healing intention to that patient. Each healer would then receive a new patient until every patient had been treated by every healer.

By the end of the study, all ten patients in the treated group were still alive and in far better condition than the control population, 40 percent of whom had already died. A second study, doubling the size of the experimental group, produced the same decisive results.[17]

In her book, McTaggart describes some of the other "150 studies, varying in scientific rigor,"[18] which have been done on remote healing. Some have used Western healers, some Eastern; some have utilized prayer, some meditators; some have involved groups; and all have utilized intention.

As with my own work, consistent indicators of healing success include: beginning a treatment with a clear intention to heal; an altered state of consciousness; an ability to bring the brain into peak focus; a sense of unity with the person or organism to be healed; a sense of being in touch with an external source of power; and a shedding of the ego in order to get out of the way.

The Quantum Effect

The study of quantum physics—the inner structure of atoms, which make up everything in the physical world—has decisively undermined materialistic science's claim to present a complete description of reality. Objects are not composed of pellets of matter, as scientists once thought, but of nonmaterial packets of energy called "quanta" or "particles." Tables and oranges and even people are therefore not material things, but concentrated fields of energy that appear solid only because of the crudeness of our senses.

In the weird inner world of the atom, researchers have discovered that quanta have no ability to act individually, but only as part of a field. If you a shoot a bullet at a target, you can predict where it will strike if you know all the physical factors involved. By contrast, if you propel a particle, it's impossible to know where it will strike, no matter how much you know about it. However, if you propel a bunch of particles, you can predict a statistical pattern according to the laws of probability. In other words, causes in the quantum world do not produce individual effects. Instead, it's the interaction of a whole field that produces a probable result.

Quantum physicists have also found that total objectivity in the laboratory, without recognizing the influence of consciousness, is an illusion. For example, if two electrons become entangled in a partnership, one will always spin clockwise while the other spins counterclockwise. What determines the direction of rotation of either particle? The act of measuring it. The physicist's consciousness creates the result—what is known as the "observer effect."

Typically, electrons travel in orbits and waves of probability, which offer an infinite number of possibilities. It's our observation that causes a probability wave to collapse, thus creating an event. This suggests that human consciousness, individually and collectively, creates what we call "reality."

Once a pair of electrons becomes entangled, they remain so interconnected that they continue to act as one even when separated by space. If a physicist in London measures the spin of one of the pair, determining that its rotation is clockwise, its partner in New York will instantaneously be found rotating counterclockwise, or vice versa. This effect— what Einstein called "spooky action at a distance"—occurs no matter how great the electrons' seperation. It has created one of the greatest puzzles in quantum physics: how can a particle know faster than the speed of light the direction of rotation assumed by its partner so that it will always spin in the opposite direction? Once again we have an effect akin to human telepathy.

These findings are not mere abstractions designed to tease the minds of fuzzy-headed theorists. Quantum processes underlie such useful inventions as the transistor, the laser, and the microchip. And since everything in our sensory world, including ourselves, is made up of quanta, it's reasonable to assume that these principles also operate in the physical world.

Communication-at-a-distance, the power of conscious intention, and quantum-field effects are critical to energy healing. Though these principles have been proven in the laboratory, Western culture has not yet incorporated them into everyday thinking. When we do, energy healing will not seem like such a stretch.

NOTES

Chapter 5: The Sorcerer's Apprentice

1. Ruth Montgomery, *A Search for the Truth* (New York: Fawcett, 1985).

2. Bernard Grad, "The Dynamics of Healing: Altered States, Ritual, and Medicine" (lecture, American Society of Psychical Research, New York, NY, April 7, 1991); "An Anatomy of Healing," *ASPR Newsletter* 18, no. 1:2; and "Some Biological Effects of the Laying On of Hands: A Review of Experiments with Animals and Plants," *Journal of the American Society for Psychical Research* 59: 95–127.

3. Grad, "The Dynamics of Healing"; "An Anatomy of Healing"; and "Some Biological Effects."

4. Smith's research is discussed in: Richard Gerber, *Vibrational Medicine: New Choices for Healing Ourselves* (Santa Fe, NM: Bear & Co., 1988), 299–300.

5. Dolores Krieger, "Therapeutic Touch: The Imprimatur of Nursing," *American Journal of Nursing* 75, no. 5 (May 1975): 784–87.

Chapter 6: Crossroads

1. Leonard J. Lerner, Albert Bianchi, and Margaret Dzelzkalns, "Effect of Hydroxyurea on Growth of a Transplantable Mouse Mammary

Adenocarcinoma," *Cancer Research* 26 (November 1966): 2297–2300; and Charles River Laboratories, "A Catalog of In-Vitro Cell Lines, Transplantable Animal and Human Tumors and Microarrays," (Frederick, MD: National Cancer Institute, 2010).

Chapter 9: Enigmas

1. Bernard Grad, "Healing by the Laying On of Hands: Review of Experiments and Implications," *Pastoral Psychology* 21 (1970): 19–26.

Chapter 10: Time Out

1. Russell Targ and Harold Putoff, *Mind-Reach: Scientists Look at Psychic Abilities* (New York: Dell, 1978).

Chapter 11: More Moonlighting with Mice

1. William F. Bengston and David Krinsley, "The Effect of the 'Laying On of Hands' on Transplanted Breast Cancer in Mice," *Journal of Scientific Exploration* 14, no. 3 (Fall 2000): 353–364.

2. Andrew Greeley, *The Sociology of the Paranormal,* Studies in Religion and Ethnicity, vol. 3 (Beverly Hills, CA: Sage Publications, 1975).

3. Bernie Siegel, *Love, Medicine and Miracles: Lessons Learned about Self-Healing from a Surgeon's Experience with Exceptional Patients* (New York: Harper & Row, 1986).

Chapter 13: Eureka!

1. Henry K. Beecher, "The Powerful Placebo," *Journal of the American Medical Association* 159, no. 17 (1955): 1602–1606.

2. Andrew Weil, *Health and Healing* (Boston: Houghton Mifflin, 1983).

3. William F. Bengston and Margaret M. Moga, "Resonance, Placebo Effects, and Type II Errors: Some Implications from Healing Research for Experimental Methods," *Journal of Alternative and Complementary Medicine* 13, no. 3 (May 2007): 317–327.

Chapter 14: Talking to Machines

1. William F. Bengston, Margaret M. Moga, "Resonance, Placebo Effects, and Type II Errors: Some Implications from Healing Research for

Experimental Methods," *Journal of Alternative and Complementary Medicine* 13, no. 3 (May 2007): 317–327.

2. William F. Bengston, Margaret M. Moga, "Anomalous DC Magnetic Field Activity during a Bioenergy Healing Experiment," forthcoming in *Journal of Scientific Exploration.*

3. Luke Hendricks, William Bengston, Jay Gunkelman, "The Healing Connection: EEG Harmonics, Entrainment, and Schumann's Resonances," *Journal of Scientific Exploration.*

Chapter 15: "Why Haven't You Won a Nobel Prize?"

1. Dolores Krieger, "Therapeutic Touch: The Imprimatur of Nursing," *American Journal of Nursing* 75, no. 5 (May 1975): 784–87.

2. From the author's personal copy of The Holy Bible, King James Version, 1611, British and Foreign Bible Society (London: Cambridge University Press, no publication date).

3. Rahn's quote is cited in: W. Edward Mann, *Orgone, Reich, and Eros: Wilhelm Reich's Theory of Life Energy* (New York: Touchstone Books, Simon and Schuster, 1973), 106.

Appendix B: Research Guide

1. Robert G. Jahn and Brenda J. Dunne, "The PEAR Proposition," *Journal of Scientific Exploration* 19, no. 2 (2005): 195–245.

2. Peter Tompkins and Christopher Bird, *The Secret Life of Plants* (New York: Harper & Row, 1973).

3. Backster's ridicule is discussed in: Lynne McTaggart, *The Intention Experiment: Using Your Thoughts to Change Your Life and the World* (New York: Free Press, 2008), 40.

4. The Miller/Worrall experiment is discussed in: Richard Gerber, *Vibrational Medicine: New Choices for Healing Ourselves* (Santa Fe, NM: Bear & Co., 1988), 313–14.

5. Wallace's theory is discussed in: Richard M. Restak, MD, *The Brain: The Last Frontier* (New York: Warner Books, 1980) 76–7, 87.

6. Alistair Hardy, "Biology and Psychical Research," *Proceedings of the Society for Psychical Research* 50, no. 183 (1953).

7. See: Lyall Watson, *Supernature: A Natural History of the Supernatural* (London: Sceptre, an imprint of Hodder and Stoughton Paperbacks, 1986), 249–50.

8. Insect communication is discussed in: Colin Wilson, *The Occult* (London: Grafton Books, 1979), 159–63.

9. Rupert Sheldrake, *A New Science of Life: the Hypothesis of Formative Causation* (Los Angeles: J. P. Tarcher Inc., 1987), 186–9.

10. McDougall's rat experiments are discussed in Sheldrake, *A New Science of Life*, 186–9.

11. Émile Durkheim, *Suicide: A Study in Sociology*, ed. George Simpson, trans. John A. Spaulding (New York: Free Press, 1997).

12. Suicide statistics are from the Centers for Disease Control's National Center for Health Statistics: *cdc.gov/nchs*

13. The Bastyr University study is cited in: McTaggart, *The Intention Experiment*, 51.

14. The Mexico City study is cited in: McTaggart, *The Intention Experiment*, 50–2.

15. McTaggart, *The Intention Experiment*, 32.

16. Green's findings are cited in: McTaggart, *The Intention Experiment*, 23–4.

17. Targ's study is cited in: McTaggart, *The Intention Experiment*, 47–8.

18. McTaggart, *The Intention Experiment*, xxvii.

ABOUT THE AUTHOR

WILLIAM F. BENGSTON is a professor of sociology at St. Joseph's College in New York. His areas of specialization include research methods and statistics. For twenty years, Dr. Bengston has been doing research into anomalous healing and has published numerous articles in the *Journal of Scientific Exploration,* the *Journal of Alternative and Complementary Medicine,* and *Explore: The Journal of Science and Healing.* In addition, he has lectured throughout the United States and Europe. His research has produced the first successful full cures of transplanted mammary cancer and methylcholanthrene-induced sarcomas in experimental mice by laying-on-of-hands techniques that he helped to develop. He has also investigated assorted correlates to healing such as geomagnetic micropulsations,

EEG harmonics, and entrainment. Dr. Bengston is the elected president for the Society for Scientific Exploration. For more information, see bengstonresearch.com or contact info@bengstonresearch.com.

ABOUT SOUNDS TRUE

Sounds True was founded in 1985 to disseminate spiritual wisdom. Located in Boulder, Colorado, Sounds True is a multimedia publisher of some of the leading teachers and visionaries of our time. We strive with every title to preserve the essential "living wisdom" of the author, artist, or spiritual teacher. It is our goal to create products that provide information to a reader or listener, and that embody the essential quality of a wisdom transmission.

To receive a free catalog, visit SoundsTrue.com, call toll-free 800-333-9185, or write to us at the address below.

P.O. Box 8010
Boulder CO 80306